David
Byrne

BY **JOHN HOWELL**

PHOTOGRAPHS BY *f*- STOP FITZGERALD

Thunder's
Mouth
Press

New
York

A BALLIETT & FITZGERALD BOOK

Acknowledgements:

Thanks to Lori Somes, who was the first to think this book could really
happen; Victoria Rose, who gave encouragement at a crucial time; Sarah
Caplan, whose patience and good will was a miracle; and to David Byrne, who
came through with the goods in more than one tight spot.

Thanks, at Thunder's Mouth, to Neil Ortenberg for his vision and faith,
and to Anne Stillwaggon for her guidance and patience; we would also like to
thank Madeleine Morel for performing the marriage.—B&F

First Edition.
First printing, 1992.

Published by Thunder's Mouth Press
54 Green Street, Suite 4S, New York, NY 10013

Distributed by:
Publisher's Group West
4065 Hollis Street
Emeryville, CA 94608
(800)788-3123

Series editor: f-stop fitzgerald
Editorial director: Will Balliett
Line / copy editor: Duncan Bock
Series book design: Frank Olinsky
Graphic artist: Beatrice Schafroth
Graphic production: Linda Rubes

Howell, John
David Byrne / by John Howell: with
photographs by f-stop Fitzgerald. —1st ed.
p.   cm.   (American Originals)
Includes the author's interviews with David Byrne.
Discography: p.
Filmography: p.
Includes bibliographical references.
ISBN 1-56025-031-3 : $11.95
1. Byrne, David, 1952 -
2. Rock musicians—United States—
Biography. I. Byrne, David, 1952-   II. Title.   III. Series.
ML410.B997H7   1992
780' .92—dc20
[B]
91-45306
CIP
MN

Dedication

To my three graces: Laura, Julia, and Fiona.

C O N T E N T S

9   **David Byrne: Man in Media**
An introductory biographical essay by John Howell.

37   **Artist in Dialogue**
David Byrne and John Howell discuss the artist's
working process.

91   **New Release**
A selection of original photographs taken by David Byrne while
on tour.

105   **Rei Momo Tour Diary**
An excerpt from the diary kept by David Byrne while on tour in
North and South America.

141   **Timeline**
A complete, chronological discography, filmography, videogra-
phy, and list of publications.

MAN IN MEDIA

BY JOHN HOWELL

WHO IS DAVID BYRNE? In the course of our conversations over the past two years, I got the feeling that it is a question he poses to himself with refreshing regularity.

A polymath, whose ideas stretch across fields (music, art, film, theater), media (performance, recording, books, photography), and even cultures (outsider art, Yoruba practices in Bahia, Haitian *vodun*), the former singer/songwriter for Talking Heads has made a point of indulging his curiosity wherever it leads. And yet, he has shown how disparate ideas can be pulled together by a disciplined, singular point of view in projects that overlap and feed off each other—with an unexpected ease. The embodiment of the point at which pop culture meets the SoHo aesthetic, Byrne is the artist as restless collector, roaming through multiple cultures and media for clues about how to better express the complexity of modern life.

It's no accident that David Byrne has long been settled in New York's SoHo district, the roughly twenty-square-block area which has been a nerve center of new ideas and trends in the arts, fashion and design since the early seventies. Packed with art galleries, performance spaces, specialty bookshops and hip restaurants, it is a pool of energized thought and activity, in and out of which he likes to dip, in the process of nourishing his own brainstorms.

The living quarters of his loft clearly reflect eclectic interests.

African statues stand near a bedroom area set off with Japanese translucent sliding-partitions. Books on Afro-Brazilian art are stacked next to film studies. And against a wall is his idea center, a desk surrounded by cassettes, videotapes, film scripts and drawings. A relatively new addition are the toys scattered about; Byrne and his wife, Adelle "Bonny" Lutz, are the parents of Malu Valentine, an active two-year-old.

The other half of the large space, which also contains a kitchen, is set up as a work area, with desks for assistants and racks of shelves for archives. One back room contains the typical tools of a contemporary musician: computers and electronic equipment, plus a couple of keyboards and guitars. Another storeroom holds boxes of unsorted and unexhibited photographs—Byrne's own version of sketchbooks (a random sampling produces a box of shots of light fixtures from around the world, taken on a year-long tour).

It is the well-used space of a working artist.

In person, Byrne is basically shy, (a trait surprisingly common in performing artists). Participating in a conversation such as the one which follows in this book, he thinks long and carefully before answering; you learn to wait for a response. He often qualifies, extends or circles back to a thought, as if thinking about a question or idea for the first time. He will not be cornered into making certain kinds of statements (particularly about what audiences think he should be doing). Unfailingly courteous, he remains reserved, growing animated most often when discussing whatever ideas he's interested in at the moment. He laughs abruptly, often at unexpected moments, triggered by a sudden absurdity—he has a very developed sense of incongruity. And he wears his celebrity lightly, although walking the streets with him can be jarring for anyone not used to being stared at or constantly approached by strangers who launch into serious conversations.

As I began this project—a mid-career "snapshot" of David Byrne's working process—having been casually aquainted with him for over a decade, I kept thinking about our very first meeting, when he made his initial appearance on the stage of SoHo. Looking back, I realized that his path has been remarkably consistent from the start, and it is in that beginning that the roots of his work today can be seen.

II

On a cool March night in 1976, the lights went up for another concert at the Kitchen in New York City. Located in SoHo, a thriving avant-garde arts scene, the Kitchen had begun in 1971 as a center set up exclusively for the alternative performing arts, including experimental music, dance, theater, video, and that catchall category called performance art. It took its name from its first location, in the former kitchen of the Broadway Central Hotel, an ancient building— it later collapsed—that had been converted into an arts center. In 1973 the Kitchen moved to SoHo, where artists of all types were beginning to exhibit and perform in Civil War-era industrial buildings.

Like others in the space's core audience of a few hundred, I went to the Kitchen regularly, drawn by its new and different programs. Pop culture in the mid-seventies was disco and *Jaws,* things you knew all too well. The fact that you didn't know what to expect at a Kitchen performance was part of the thrill of being there.

The event that March night was billed as a music concert by a group called Talking Heads, about whom almost nothing was known except that they had attended the Rhode Island School of Design, an art school, and had performed at CBGB's, a decrepit club on the Bowery which had begun presenting bands playing strange kinds of rock-and-roll . The glare of the spotlights (or rather the clamp lamps that passed for lighting equipment) on the stageless, performing area at one end of the loft space revealed a rock band's instruments: drum kit, an electric bass, several guitars, a microphone, and amplifiers. This standard power trio setup looked strangely out of place at the Kitchen, where most music concerts were so deliberately experimental that they often avoided the use of anything like regular musical instruments.

This notion of the familiar turned strange continued when a trio of unlikely looking rockers filed in: a curly-haired, cherub-faced man who took a seat at the drums; a slender, blonde, freckled woman who picked up the bass; and a tall, skinny man who, in what would quickly become a cliché, resembled a cross between Ralph Nader and Anthony Perkins, and who planted himself (with his guitar) in front of the microphone. The band members looked like the students they had been until shortly before that. They were dressed casually, as if they had simply walked out of their dorm rooms and into the spotlight.

When the band began to play, it became clear that their music was as skewed as their anti-rock appearance. It was similar to rock, but it certainly wasn't rock as we knew it then. The rhythms stuttered rather than rolled; the tempos were quirky, too fast and jerky for dancing; the bass wove in and out of the songs' structures rather than generating a groove; and the lyrics, as best they could be deciphered from the singer's strangled, high-pitched delivery, were dense and abstract, not at all like pop song verses and choruses.

The way Talking Heads performed completed this double-take. The group resembled clean-cut suburban kids, going about their business in a matter-of-fact manner. Standing stock still and saying almost nothing between songs except to announce the titles, the band sped through a set with none of the exuberant abandon of rock-and-rollers. Instead, they seemed to concentrate on simply presenting the songs, on creating a zone of musical dialogue in which they would meet the attention of the audience halfway. Neither did they match the look or sound of the experimentalists who usually performed at the Kitchen: somber men and women with neo-academic airs, fiddling with banks of electronic gadgets to create sound environments or presenting esoteric techniques such as Tibetan chanting in concerts that seemed like secular religious ceremonies.

As Talking Heads's concert went on, the attention focused increasingly on the lead singer and guitarist, David Byrne, partly because of his unlikely front man attributes: science nerd looks, awkward poses, and That Voice—a choked tenor. His singing voice was the vocal equivalent of nervously clenching and twisting hands. Through it, he phrased dozens of sentences packed with odd thoughts, offbeat perceptions, banal clichés, and verbal fragments that didn't follow the laws of pop song lyrics—they didn't rhyme, were polysyllabic, and didn't repeat key words and phrases often or in the right places. The sensibility they revealed was at once naive and alienated, deadpan and angst-riddled.

The concert resembled performance art; familiar cultural forms were turned upside down to shake loose new meanings. In performance art the gesture was all; it was only necessary to sketch the outlines of the subjects, not to actually fill them out. The underlying structures and ideas were thought to be the truly important element. Performance art also blurred the line between genres, between public and private, persona and person, staged act and behavior. It was the performing cousin of conceptual art, a movement that pioneered

The big-band, punk-funk Talking Heads, featuring Nona Hendryx and Adrian Belew.

the notion of art as idea, rather than "mere" experience.

Yet odd as it was, Talking Heads's performance was a compelling one, holding the audience's attention in delighted suspension as only genuinely original art can do. It was like rock, but smarter. And while it was artful, it had something of the energy and fun—the sexiness—of rock.

It turned out that the group did indeed think of their presentation as an art concept. In the Kitchen's catalogue for that year, published later in the summer, Talking Heads described themselves as "a group of performing artists whose medium is rock-and-roll and the pursuant 'band' organization and visual presentation. The original music and lyrics are structured within the commercial accessibility of rock-and-roll sound and contemporary, popular language. Lead singer Byrne relies on Chris Frantz and Tina Weymouth to complete their anti-individualist stance as a group concept."

Today, David Byrne is known worldwide as a singer, composer, and musician, and also as a film and video director, visual artist, designer, record label producer, photographer, and ethnographer. He has played on records that have sold in the millions, has won an Oscar (for his contribution to the score for *The Last Emperor*), and has videos he directed in the collection of the Museum of Modern Art in New York. While it strikes some as peculiar or even pretentious that a rock star works in so many media and roles, it's clear that the roots of Byrne's singular, category-defying vision lie as far back as Talking Heads's earliest public shows. What sort of artist would choose a rock band as his initial vehicle for a radical take on contemporary culture? And manage to make that band a major force in world music, to boot? And then, go beyond Talking Heads to become an innovative solo artist, collaborating with major figures in several fields?

III

The roots of Byrne's artistic stance go back to his personal beginnings. Born in Dumbarton, Scotland, in 1952, he was raised in Baltimore from the second grade. To this day, he maintains a United Kingdom passport, a literal reminder of what seems like a deeply ingrained "outsider" attitude. It's not hard to see the indirect influences on Byrne's subsequent career of Baltimore's other, older generation of distinctive artists—the ordinary-life-turned-perversely-upside-down humor of filmmaker John Waters, and the high art seriousness of composer Philip Glass; the first an ultimate outsider in the world of commercial film, the second, the consummate art world insider. Early on, Byrne was the class cut-up; as a teenager, he performed "aggressive" songs on the ukulele at college coffeehouses. In 1970, torn between his interests in art and science (his father was an electrical engineer), Byrne chose art and signed up for RISD in Providence, Rhode Island. He lasted one year, then spent another year at Maryland Institute's College of Art in Baltimore before dropping out of college entirely. While in school, his interests ran toward conceptual art activities, such as passing out questionnaires, making disposable Xerox art, and taking lots of Polaroid snapshots which he put together in collages. Collective art groups then active in New York, such as Art & Language, reduced art to the status of printed declarations laden with philosphical jargon tacked to gallery walls. They fascinated Byrne. "I thought it was the ultimate in eliminating all the superfluous stuff in art and being left with nothing but the idea," he said.

Though no longer a student, he returned to RISD to hang out with a friend, Chris Frantz, who was still enrolled there. The duo formed a band called the Artistics (quickly nicknamed the Autistics for their energetic but ragged playing) which performed "loud rock." For Frantz, who had been a drummer in various bands since high school, playing in the Artistics was a natural activity. For Byrne, it was the start of an insight: Rock might be a useful vehicle for his ideas.

By 1975, Byrne, Frantz, and Frantz's girlfriend, Tina Weymouth, another RISD student, were living together in a tumble-down, cold-water loft in lower Manhattan and playing as a trio called Talking Heads, a term suggested by a friend, which referred to TV lingo for head shots of people talking. Weymouth had never played bass but that was considered a plus for their mutual project, something between rock and what was then generically called "new music."

The basic idea was startling in its simplicity: "The image we present along with our songs is what we are really like," went the band's early promotional copy. Intent on collapsing the distance between art and life, Talking Heads decided not to dress up, not to perform bravura drum and guitar solos, and not to pander to the audience. In other words, they would be rockers but not rock stars. "We were

Talking Heads keyboard player Jerry Harrison.

going to honestly present what we do," explained Byrne, "tearing it down to the bare bones."

This notion found a home in the freewheeling atmosphere of CBGB's, the Bowery club that had begun presenting a new brand of rock that took its attitude from British punk, its energy from a determination to reclaim pop music from disco, and its art smarts from the interchange between artists, writers, and musicians. Talking Heads soon became regulars, sharing bills with the punk-parodist Ramones, the all-attitude Blondie, the poetry-ranting Patti Smith, and the guitar-warrior Television driven by Tom Verlaine's Rimbaud-esque looks and rhapsodic guitar duets with Richard Lloyd. (Verlaine, who also hailed from Maryland, was the original force behind CBGB's new rock).

The atmosphere at CBGB's was contagious; soon bona fide visual artists were playing in rock bands as well as using them for inspiration. (Robert Longo was one; he would later execute a huge wall construction, punningly titled "Heads Will Roll," that featured a life-size cutout silhouette of Byrne). In fact, SoHo at this time was like one great art party, and Byrne was right in the middle of it, beginning his artistic jaywalk between high and low art.

He didn't have much money (someone at the Kitchen once borrowed a dollar from me to lend to Byrne, who needed something to eat). Like many of us, he worked at odd jobs (movie usher, photo lab assistant) to support himself. And he dressed like an overage high school student—polo shirts, jeans, sneakers—with social manners that were awkward but charming. My memory of many of the events of that time—new dance and music concerts, art exhibitions, performance art shows, and downtown rock concerts—include a quiet Byrne, usually standing off to the side, taking it all in.

Tagged the "Republicans of rock" for their deliberately low-key, preppie-esque performances, the band members soon became a distinctive presence by just being their unassuming selves, almost incidentally creating the music and audience for what would become today's college-based music scene. They did this simply via their choice to be what they were: college grads with some radical ideas. During the birth of rock-and-roll in the fifties, school had been a symbol to rebel against. In the sixties, rockers were still dropouts and rebels. Talking Heads made school okay by opening up the conventions of rock to at least acknowledge what was a salient fact in most middle-class experience.

Usually appearing in T-shirts and jeans, simply standing and playing and singing, they built up a repertory of songs with a similarly stripped-down, anti-drama air to them. "I wanted to make boring things seem dramatic, instead of dramatic things seem boring," Byrne said. Tunes like "Don't Worry About the Government" and "Found a Job" talked about ordinary life in a droll, deadpan way within the terse format of rock song structures.

One of their songs was different. "Psycho Killer" was the first song Byrne ever wrote, when he was in the Artistics and listening to "some Alice Cooper songs." As performed by Talking Heads, it became the group's first popular number; it is still one of the most compelling of Byrne's compositions. Byrne admitted to using another strategy in coming up with the song: "I wondered if you took those overly dramatic subjects and, in a sensitive way, wrote from inside the person's mind, would it work?" The interior point of view in "Psycho Killer" allowed the true nuttiness of its sociopathic character to come through, with its peculiarly haunting, partly French refrain of "Psycho killer, *qu'est-ce que c'est*/Run, run, run, run away." With typical offhand reasoning, Byrne claimed that it was a "natural delusion that a psychotic killer would imagine himself as very refined and use a foreign language to talk to himself." By being nonjudgmental about a sensational subject, and by using the unexpected twist of speaking French to further distance the horror, Byrne tightened the anxiety to a high-tension pitch.

"Tense" would be too low-key a way to describe his performance, in which his Anthony Perkins looks and demeanor played into a *Psycho* allusion, an inescapable reference that Byrne heightened through his skewed performance. "I remember that I was projecting a sense of heartfelt sincerity," he has said of films of his early performances. "It was like I was trying to invest a lot of heart and emotion into the material, and, as it turned out, it looks like I'm really angst-ridden." That combination of intended earnestness and accidental turmoil especially served "Psycho Killer," which, as seen at the usual one a.m. showtime in the dank, rowdy confines of CBGB's, became a cult rite, the seventies version of experiencing the Doors playing "The End" in the sixties at the Whiskey A Go-Go in L.A.

By 1977, the year following their foray into the Kitchen, the band was at a crossroads: Their ambitions were growing more rapidly than their ability to realize them. Byrne couldn't carry the whole load

Virtuoso guitarist Adrian Belew added depth to the big-band sound during The Name of This Band is Talking Heads tour.

vocally, the band was adamant that Weymouth not sing back-up (so she wouldn't be perceived as just another decorative female), and the arrangements were too thin. In search of some musical solutions, the three founders took on a fourth member, Jerry Harrison. A Harvard architecture student, Harrison had been playing with the Modern Lovers, a group whose leader, Jonathan Richman, was even quirkier and more concerned about being "himself" than Byrne. Harrison's combination of a serious academic background and offbeat musical experience made him a perfect fit. Originally looking for a keyboard player to push a sketchy sound closer to rock as the band prepared to record their first album of songs, Talking Heads soon discovered Harrison's versatility. He moved back and forth between guitars, keyboards, and other instruments, and sang back-up, which made it possible to fill out the group's arrangements. Harrison joined the band for some downtown club concerts which set off the first of several successive critical tempests about Talking Heads: Was a more "musical" approach diluting the band's originality?

After the band's first album, another addition had a profound impact on their direction. Brian Eno—a founding member of the English art-rock band Roxy Music and a musical theorist best known for combining Satie and electronics into what he called "ambient music," a kind of postmodern Muzak—became an unofficial fifth band member. More an idea resource than an actual musician, his work as producer with Talking Heads began with their second album, *More Songs About Buildings and Food*, and continued through the next two (*Fear of Music, Remain in Light*). He had two important effects on the band's goals. His notion of music as "found sound" showed Byrne, by now established as the band's songwriter, another way to compose: by juxtaposition, distortion, and chance assemblage. And Eno's fanatic interest in Third World music, especially African and Middle Eastern rhythms, would push Talking Heads into a polyrhythmic, groove-building mode. When these influences were combined with the band's natural affinity for James Brown-derived funk and soul, the result was a thickly textured, driving sound, pushed by layers of propulsive drums and bass, percussively strummed guitars, and rhythm-filling keyboards over which Byrne's wailing lyrics floated—a hybrid like nothing heard before.

And it contained a new role for Byrne. The band's cover of Al Green's "Take Me to the River" created a different persona for him as a performer: the singer as a preacher-shaman. It was a role he would also explore with Eno in their collaborative *My Life in the Bush of Ghosts*, an album of manipulated found voices and sounds (taken from radio broadcasts, for example) which merged into something like a cacophony of radio evangelists' rantings set to rhythms from around the world. As an attitude, the role also began to infiltrate Byrne's already cryptic, fragmented lyrics; it was a way to project honest passion with an edge of absurdist humor.

"I was coming to accept the idea that rational thinking has its limits," Byrne says now. (This neo-soulman/preacher persona would culminate in Byrne's direct takeoff on the forehead smacking and possessed staggering of Ernest Angley—the Liberace of televangelists—in *Stop Making Sense*, the 1984 Talking Heads concert film.) The widespread radio airplay that "Take Me to the River" received throughout 1978 brought the band a larger, commercial audience; that it completed a conceptual loop—from radio-style singing/preaching back to radio broadcast—surely satisfied Byrne's intellectual notions just as much as the contradiction of an art-rock band becoming a widely popular phenomenon.

The Afro-funk tilt of Talking Heads's music continued to develop until it became clear that a four-piece band could no longer play the music they were creating. Thus was born the expanded, racially and sexually integrated Talking Heads, unveiled in the late summer of 1980 at Heatwave, a one-day festival of "new wave" rock held outside Toronto. Adding a wraparound group of talented musicians and singers, all but one of whom were black, and melding them seamlessly into the arrangements and performances (there were no supporting parts), Talking Heads suddenly became a progressive political statement as well as an innovative rock band. Without exactly setting out to strike such a stance, Talking Heads found that their ideas about rock and how it should be made had led them to a social situation that was naturally sophisticated.

The band responded cautiously to characterizations of their politics, as if to say that doing the right thing was indeed natural. But the evolution of Talking Heads was inevitably colored by the start of the Reagan era, a period that was clearly not going to be about innovation and social equality.

By the time the new lineup hit the stage of Radio City Music Hall in New York, Talking Heads was a popular as well as an intellectual success story, with an audience made up of downtown artists, new wave musicians, and pop music fans. Of course, there were arguments about whether the band's turn to the roots of rock was reactionary or not, whether a once stringently conceptual project was becoming merely entertaining. But that first night, the quibblers were buried under an unanswerable retort: Just feel that groove! Without sacrificing their distinctive ideas, Talking Heads had become a thoroughly persuasive band.

They also had a hit single. With "Once in a Lifetime" (from the *Remain in Light* album) Byrne further transformed the preacher persona. "I'd been listening to some preachers on the radio," he explains. "I adopted the character of a preacher and kind of spontaneously spurted out the lyrics that became the verses." The repetitive, rhetorical questions with metaphysical implications ("How did I get here?") coupled with a rolling, rousing beat to make the tune into a musical experience that moved the feet as well as the consciousness. "The excitement or release that I thought was possible from music became a reality. It became impossible not to dance around to it on stage."

Byrne's two obsessions of the moment, dance and African rhythms, then came together in an unexpected way when choreographer Twyla Tharp asked him to create music for a full-length narrative ballet called *The Catherine Wheel*. Tharp had been using Talking Heads records as exercise music for her dance company; having created shorter dances to songs by Chuck Berry, the Beach Boys, Bruce Springsteen, and Supertramp, she began an outline for a dance about "a horrible family" with the idea that Byrne's roiling rhythms and quirky lyrics would match her disjunctive movement. At the time, Byrne was reading a book by John Chernoff, *African Rhythm and African Sensibility*, concerning the political, social, and spiritual meanings of the music, and providing many examples of what Chernoff had learned in ten years of studying African drumming. Byrne enlisted Chernoff in the ballet project. (Chernoff is credited as co-author of the suite's standout number, "Big Business," in which African-style "galloping" guitar was introduced for perhaps the first time in Western pop.) Working with Brian Eno as well, Byrne produced a ninety-minute score of eleven songs.

The Catherine Wheel opened on Broadway in the fall of 1981, and was instantly acclaimed as a major dance-theater creation. Its success would have two opposite effects on Byrne's career. The meshing of a postmodern lyric sensibility with an ancient musical tradition helped push Talking Heads towards the perfectly conceived, flawlessly executed *Speaking in Tongues*, a million-plus selling album that stands as a landmark in the short history of contemporary pop as "world music." But the experience also confirmed that Byrne could work on a big scale with noted collaborators—theater directors and choreographers whose references were to visual art, as well as avant-garde dance, music, and performance art—and could produce work that satisfied the requirements of high art, not just the commercial pressures of pop music.

First would come a summary of Talking Heads's entire career to date, in the 1984 Jonathan Demme-directed concert film, *Stop Making Sense*. Conceived for the stage by Byrne, the performance layered together elements of every theatrical influence he had absorbed: Robert Wilson-style imagistic theater, performance art, television evangelism, Kabuki theater, Broadway lighting effects, and contemporary dance. Combined with the Afro-funk rhythms and superb musicianship of the expanded Talking Heads, Demme captured a band not only anthologizing but re-interpreting its history. Beginning with a solo performance of "Psycho Killer" to the accompaniment of a boom box and ending with rousing performances of "Life During Wartime" and "Take Me to the River" by the eight-piece band, *Stop Making Sense* was a major re-imagining of the idea of Talking Heads. It was a look back at history through the filters of the moment, as if this version was where the group had always intended to arrive.

Throughout the film Byrne was its central figure, moving through a catalogue of his bizarre dances: "spastic," "duck," "knock-knee," "Indian-Snake," "guitar," "possession," "vibration," "jogging," "leaning back," "wiggle." Byrne crouched, ran, staggered, marched, and squatted; he smacked his forehead á la Ernest Angley. He danced with a lamp and paraded in a huge white suit that engulfed his figure. Early in the film, he asked "Anybody have any questions?" in a flashback to his days as a conceptual artist who passed out questionnaires. His multiple role-playing in the movie was noted when he was awarded a Video Vanguard award by MTV: "He has taken the concert film from the pedestrian to the sublime by directing, composing, and dancing; a man with a style all of his own." The only problem with the performance captured on film is that it seemed so complete, so realized, that it seemed to leave Talking Heads with nowhere to go.

Drummer Chris Frantz with Talking Heads at the Warfield Theater in San Francisco.

By this time, Frantz and Weymouth had scored dance-music hits ("Genius of Love" and "Wordy Rappinghood") and a hit album with Tom Tom Club, and Harrison had released his own album of carefully arranged, new wave rock (*The Red and the Black*).

Byrne stepped up his activities away from the group too. In the next few years he would collaborate with a Who's Who of the avant-garde: composer Philip Glass, theater directors Robert Wilson and JoAnne Akalaitis, and film directors Bernardo Bertolucci and Jonathan Demme. For each, he came up with something different, as if he were testing to see just how many styles it was possible to assimilate and synthesize: a Latin song, "Loco de Amore," for Demme's film comedy, *Something Wild;* a hymn-like anthem, "Open the Kingdom," for Glass's anthology of songs, *Songs from Liquid Days;* a disjunctive, edgy score for Akalaitis's film version of her stage play, *Dead End Kids;* and minimalist neo-orientalisms for his part of the score to Bertolucci's Oscar-winning epic film, *The Last Emperor.*

His work with Wilson was the most substantial of these forays into the world of contemporary performing art. Byrne had watched Wilson's slow-moving, epic-scale stage shows since 1975, when the avant-gardist's *A Letter for Queen Victoria* had been presented on Broadway. Wilson's idea of theater as a virtually wordless dumb show—a visual tableaux of finely detailed design—had struck a chord in Byrne. Joined by Japanese choreographer Suzushi Hanayagi, the two began to work on *The Knee Plays,* a series of *entr'acte*-size vignettes originally intended to link the larger sections of Wilson's mammoth five-act, twelve-hour play *the CIVIL warS.* Although it won a Pulitzer Prize, Wilson's play has never been produced in its entirety, and Byrne's contribution, a suite of instrumental music which turned traditional New Orleans brass band music on its head, along with some typically quirky texts (sometimes read by Byrne in live performances), became part of what turned out to be a successful theater piece in its own right. (*The Knee Plays* toured the world for several years.)

By 1985 the dilemma posed by Talking Heads's unexpected success had become acute: How was Byrne to avoid turning into just another rock star? As defined by the conceptual artists of the seventies, to whom Byrne traced his aesthetic allegiance, success was measured by the originality, rigor, and beauty of the ideas themselves, not by any mass popularity they might achieve. In fact, "popularity" was considered a mark of too-easy, too-obvious thinking, and was a negative counter in the incessant status-checking of the art world. The hypocrisy and above-it-all snobbism of such an attitude was evident even back then, but its power was hard to challenge. So the question of whether Byrne and Talking Heads could evade becoming what they had set out to criticize—rock stars—was not academic but one with real consequences.

One way out was to lower the stakes. Talking Heads's next record, *Little Creatures*, was a return to their original simplicity—the four Heads were the featured musicians—and to classic Heads-style rock, in which Byrne's fragmentary lyrics and the group's arrangements of jumpy rhythms articulated a wide-eyed, *faux-naif* world view. The cover featured the "outsider" art of the "Reverend" Howard Finster, an eccentic painter; the album's choice cut was a bouncy, Cajun-flavored march, "Road to Nowhere," that turned a happy, going-to-paradise gospel motif on its head ("Takin' that ride to nowhere/we'll take that ride"). *Little Creatures* marked a deliberately low key focus on basic Americana, albeit a visionary, folkish America that no doubt seemed as exotic to the Heads's urban and suburban audience as the mythic Africa that had been conjured up in earlier songs.

At the same time, there were clues that things had changed for the band, hints of how much the group was straining to recover its balance. A curious jacket photo showed band members standing stiff as dummies (just as they had on their very first album cover) while dressed in outlandishly decorative costumes, as if to say, "See, we can dress up but it doesn't change us"; and there were songs that seemed both lyrically and musically to be more willful nonsequiturs than imaginative metaphors. It all served as a subtle reminder that Byrne still looked at Talking Heads, in some sense, as a project rather than as a rock band—a project that was now threatening to lose its value to him. He seemed to measure it by a completely different standard than did its audience or, indeed, the other band members.

This subtextual dead end was by no means apparent at the time; on its release *Little Creatures* was hailed as yet another shift of attention and image for a band from whom audiences had come to expect change. Yet it must have seemed a portent to Byrne, because he chose another, more dramatic way out of the contradiction between an anti-rock stance and top-of-the-charts success by shifting to an entirely new medium: the feature film.

As a composer and musician, Byrne had developed an accretionist method; songs were pieced together from fragments, lists of words, incidental reading, free-form jams, and isolated riffs. Conceptually, he operated as a synthesizer, pulling together ideas from a wide variety of influences and interests. This way of working owed a great deal to SoHo's avant-garde theater groups, whom Byrne had been watching closely since his arrival in New York. Byrne has said that the performance work of Wilson, the Wooster Group, and Mabou Mines theater had a "general cut-and-paste construction method," in which "a lot of elements are cut and pasted together to serve an overall structure rather than a story-like conventional theater work. That's the way I write songs—collect a lot of stuff, then put it into verses and choruses."

The move to film allowed Byrne a completely new arena in which to exercise his talents, much as the context of a rock band had once served as a medium for his earlier aspirations. It was as if the only way to ensure the vitality of his ideas was to radically change the milieu in which they were played out. The pop music notion of simply repeating a signature style to be sold to a mass audience was a looming trap that Talking Heads, for all its vaunted originality, would find as difficult to negotiate as would any garage band.

The result was that Talking Heads, by now one of the most respected and successful bands in pop music, became part of Byrne's larger project, and were relegated to a literal back-up role; the band's next album would serve as a soundtrack to the film, a movie in which its members would play only cameo parts. After *True Stories*, the other Heads continued in their individual recording and producing projects but became increasingly annoyed at their lead singer and songwriter's part-time attention. (They recorded only one more album, *Naked.*) In time, this difference in what the band represented—to Byrne, one of many possible avenues for expression; to the others, a primary commitment—would eventually cause a near-terminal friction that would result in a long, indefinite hiatus in their collaboration.

True Stories focused on small-town America, the completion of a 180-degree turn away from the pan-cultural explorations which had occupied him in the previous years. (It must be remembered, however, that daily life in a Texas town is, in its way, as exotic a topic as African culture for the Scottish-born, Baltimore-raised, New York and Los Angeles-based Byrne.) For *True Stories*, Byrne worked like an amateur ethnographer, collecting weird items from sources like the *Weekly World News*, a hodge-podge tabloid of made-up and skewed oddities.

Characters were identified by such labels as "Lazy Woman" and "Lying Woman," there was a "typical" family, and the film culminated in a "celebration of specialness," which was a cross between an amateur variety show and a performance art spectacle. There was a story of sorts, but that was rendered rather secondary by Byrne's role as "The Narrator," a guide whose combination of an earnest, Mr. Rogers-like "Gee whiz, would you look at that?" naivete and an *Our Town* urge to explain, took the place of a detailed narrative. ("I guess I'm a bit like that, so I didn't feel I was really acting that much," Byrne explained.) The music, continuing the direction of *Little Creatures*, was American vernacular, ranging from gospel and country to Tex-Mex, *norteño* (a border polka form) and shopping mall Muzak.

In the first public indication of Byrne's ambivalence about where his career was going, *True Stories* was released as two records, one featuring songs from the movie performed by Talking Heads and the other a soundtrack on which characters in the movie sang and performed. Byrne also put together a book version that contained stills, storyboards, and contextual material.

As in his lyrics for Talking Heads, Byrne avoided "serious" direct statements. "In *True Stories* I stay away from loaded subjects—sex, violence, and political intrigue—because as soon as you get on those subjects, everybody already has preconceived ideas about them. I deal with stuff that's too dumb for people to have bothered to formulate opinions on." Instead, the movie was devoted to detailed looks at a very eccentric version of daily life. The result was a deadpan kind of humor that seemed particularly Byrnian: "There are very rarely any out-and-out jokes though there are lots of things that are funny," he explained. "When you watch something with that kind of humor, it's like you're slipping into a whole way of looking at things, a little world view, and it affects the way you see everything when you leave the theater."

The collision of the everyday—a fashion show in a shopping mall, a small town parade, dinner at an important citizen's house—with Byrne's skewed way of looking at things created a pseudo-documentary travelogue with a built-in double take—at once exhilarating and baffling. So distracted were audiences by the shift of medium that hardly anyone noticed that this effect was precisely the kind of contradiction around which Talking Heads had been created.

The larger arena of feature film, and the possibility for total direc-

Bass guitarist Tina Weymouth setting the backbone for Talking Heads.

torial control (Byrne wrote, directed, and acted in the movie) seemed to be an irresistible lure for Byrne. And the "star trip" triggered by the film, which emphasized his variety of roles as well as his singular vision, seemed to address him as an artist who worked in popular culture as much as a rock-and-roll media hero. In 1985 the *New York Times Magazine* published a feature story by Ken Emerson titled "David Byrne: Thinking Man's Rock Star," the first major article which dealt with his multiple artistic personalities. The next year *Time* magazine put Byrne on its cover, labeling him "Rock's Renaissance Man" and listing his artistic identities as the cover copy ("Singer, Composer, Lyricist, Guitarist, Film Director, Writer, Actor, Video Artist, Designer, Photographer"). *Time* even allowed Byrne to design his own cover image, in the form of a collage photograph, a privilege previously accorded to only one other subject, the artist Robert Rauschenberg.

The down side to feature film work had been the lengthy planning involved (*True Stories* was three years in the making) and the struggle to finance such expensive projects—not until 1992 would another Byrne feature film get a go-ahead development deal.

But Byrne also continued to keep one foot in the downtown art scene. In 1988 he and Wilson collaborated again, on *The Forest*, a theatrical conflation of the Babylonian epic of Gilgamesh and Fritz Lang's silent film classic, *Metropolis*, produced in Germany and for the Brooklyn Academy of Music's avant-performing arts series, the Next Wave festival. Byrne composed an equally oxymoronish score, one that brought together musical references as diverse as Wagner, yodeling, and neo-symphonic movie music.

Seeing Byrne and Wilson work together, one was struck by their similarities, in everything from looks to manner to aesthetic. Byrne had spent time at every Wilson show since 1975's improbable Broadway production, *A Letter for Queen Victoria*. The study paid off in *The Forest*'s score, which was stronger than usual for a Wilson piece and drove home his stylized images and tableaux. (Unfortunately, a planned film version of *The Forest*, to be directed by Byrne, fell through). By the end of the decade Byrne had cemented his art world credentials by contributing photographs to *Artforum* and *Parkett*, both cutting-edge art magazines. He also exhibited collages in Tokyo and London.

In 1987 Byrne recorded the *Naked* album with Talking Heads, an attempt to revive the black inflections of earlier records—it was recorded in Paris, using African musicians—but submerged in a mix thought to be more pop, a sort of customized "world beat" music. The sound was there but not the feel—the songs seemed distracted, less than sharply focused.

But Byrne was shifting gears again. In his personal life, he and his companion of five years, designer and actress Adelle "Bonny" Lutz were married. And then in the most dramatic shift of all, as if emboldened by the successful handling of the many roles required to produce *True Stories*, Byrne struck out on his own musically, in a major way.

His fascination with African music led him to Bahia, the northeastern province of Brazil that is primarily Yoruban in population and culture; the ancestors of contemporary Bahians were originally brought to the country as slaves where, despite horrendous conditions, they managed to create an African culture that is still going strong today. Here, Byrne located an entire belief system that expanded his ideas of what could be done with Afro-Caribbean sounds when they were mixed with pop. "If you go back in the history of American popular music," he claimed, "You're constantly finding hidden elements of Yoruba influence." Byrne was taking aim at more than a musical tradition, though: "There's a lot of beauty and spirituality in the Afro-Brazilian culture. I'm interested in the music not so much as a textural idea but as a whole different way of organizing and listening to music that leads you to the spirituality that's behind it—the force that created it in the first place."

This sense of a larger, explicitly spiritual framework marked a shift for Byrne, from Talking Heads-style earnest irony and *True Stories's* deadpan humor to a point of view that could almost be seen as a yearning for the transcendent as embodied in the exotic "other." In some sense, Talking Heads had been in search of the transcendent from the beginning. They started out looking for it in everyday epiphanies, and then continued the search in the rock-funk fusion which melded Afro-ecstasy with intellectual extremism. It now became an overt goal. Afro-Caribbean music offered rich, new possibilities; it also came complete with a culture that included a major alternate religion, Candomblé Nago, a practice organized around age-old Yoruban dance-music rituals. Byrne explored this culture in a documentary film, *Ilé Aiyé (The House of Life)* that combined straightforward recording of Candomblé ceremonies with such editing

Vocalist Nona Hendryx, formerly with Labelle, added back-up vocals and lots of fun during The Name of This Band is Talking Heads tour.

devices as intercut titles and split-screen views.

Byrne was at pains to emphasize the religion's joyous nature, its assimilation of aspects of Catholicism, its relation to rhythm and blues, gospel, and Latin music, and its reliance on music and dance—especially in percussion-driven events—to generate euphoria. *Ilé Aiyé* performed a typical Byrne straddle by being shown on public television as part of the *Alive From Off-Center* series and exhibited as part of an important international art exhibition, *Magiciens de la Terre*, held in Paris, France.

Byrne also started up a record label, Luaka Bop, which began to issue anthologies of already recorded music. *Beleza Tropical*, the first release, was put together with the help of Arto Lindsay, a new wave peer (DNA, Ambitious Lovers) who had grown up in Brazil. It was a popular as well as critical success. Other titles followed, all oriented around Afro-Latin music—a collection of sambas, two volumes of Cuban classics, and the works of Tom Zé, a contemporary Brazilian composer and musician whose work mixes tradition and innovation in a way startlingly similar to that of Talking Heads.

And most significantly, he recorded a solo album, *Rei Momo* ("King of Carnival"), which melded lyrics in his familiar style with Latin rhythms. Working with New York-based musicians from the bands of Rubén Blades, Celia Cruz, Tito Puente, and Wilfredo Vargas, and the Brazilian band Os Paralamas do Sucesso, and writing songs with well-known musicians such as Johnny Pacheco and Willie Colon, Byrne explored various styles, some familiar to Anglo Western culture—samba, rumba, merengue—and some not—pagode, cumbia, plena. The lyrics were occasionally sung in Spanish or Portuguese but the subjects and point of view were distinctively Byrnian. There were paeans to daily life ("Dirty Old Town"), almost straight romantic ballads ("I Know Sometimes a Man is Wrong"), and an anthemic call to arms ("Don't Want to Be Part of Your World"). The bulk of the songs, however, featured catchy non-sequiturs ("The Call of the Wild," "Good and Evil"). After over a decade of concentrated songwriting, Byrne still maintained that "music, lyrics, and images are most exciting when you can't quite get a handle on them."

Rei Momo was perhaps his most controversial move yet. In the early days of Talking Heads, there had been murmurs about "arty rock." During the expanded band period, some new wave critics had harped about a "retrograde" direction (a turning back to rhythm and blues which was seen in some quarters as an impediment to exploring new sounds). And, of course, Byrne had not been without critics among those who took issue with his artistic jaywalking across genres. Even his bandmates chimed in: Frustrated at not touring since 1984, Harrison, Weymouth, and Frantz appeared in 1990 as the Shrunken Heads, an obvious jibe at their absent cohort. But *Rei Momo* was released on the heels of similar musical expeditions by Paul Simon and Sting, and became part of a larger debate about a central political point: Was such border crossing just another form of colonialist ripoff?

Byrne's answers to such questions were several. For one, he was backed up by rock tradition itself (Bob Dylan sings country, David Bowie goes soul). And the "politically correct" line, that ethnicity is the determining factor, would mean—if followed to its logical end—that Byrne should be singing only Scottish folk tunes. "I'm not going to restrict myself musically because I'm only supposed to listen to whatever they think I'm supposed to listen to," Byrne said. "You can't control musicians that way. I don't think you need to have grown up with some music to be touched by it."

The most persuasive argument in Byrne's favor was an extensive live tour with a stellar band of mostly Hispanic and Brazilian musicians, including the singer Margareth Menezes. In performance, this ensemble transformed *Rei Momo*'s rough edges (a sometimes uneasy mix of choppy lyrics and gliding rhythms, plus a studio gloss of overdubbed tracks that dampened the music's inherent exuberance) into exactly what Byrne had set out to achieve: a music that combined traditional styles and a contemporary sensibiliity. Even the album's major critics were won over by the live version of *Rei Momo*. "Ecstasy is within reach," wrote Jon Pareles in the *New York Times* reviewing the show, after he had written up the album as "flat" and "studied."

At the end of 1991, in an interview with the *Los Angeles Times*, Byrne stated what had become obvious, that Talking Heads, which had not toured since 1984 or recorded since 1988's *Naked*, was on hold as a working band (a boxed set of the band's greatest hits was scheduled for a 1992 release). But on other fronts, a new feature film was finally far enough along to be mentioned as a real project, completion date unknown. Byrne also traveled to India, thinking to expand the previously exclusively Latin bias of Luaka Bop to a truly global roster; the label also issued releases by A.R. Kane, an English "house-rave" band whose conceptual psychedelicism no doubt appealed to Byrne's sensiblity, and planned to issue equally new Japanese music.

Most importantly, he recorded the typically titled *Uh-Oh*, an album that was both a step backward and forward at the same time. Although he again used many Latin musicians and sounds—especially percussion and horn charts—the overall impression was of a more natural synthesis between Afro-Caribbean instrumental styles and Talking Heads-like lyrics than on *Rei Momo*. "I've allowed a bit more of that kind of writing [Talking Heads] back into my own stuff," he explained. There was none of the diligent cataloguing of Latin rhythms, no glossary of terms, no stretches of singing in Spanish or Portuguese. The songs were a melange not unfamiliar to Talking Heads devotees, from the quirky collision of country chords and mambo rhythms in "The Cowboy Mambo" to the cryptic assemblage of clichés—from political slogans to everyday catchphrases—in "Twistin' In The Wind." There were tantalizing hints of self revelation: "People say I am strange/People say I am crazy/I don't care what people say/They can't see inside my brain," sang Byrne in "Girls On My Mind" in what sounded like an angry voice. Of course, any such earnest notions were immediately followed by deliberate silliness: "I've got girls girls girls girls on my mind," sung in a yodeling wail. As always, apparently heartfelt emotions were mixed with weird humor and a diffident, oblique stance that challenged anyone to nail down "David Byrne" in the media-mediated mix.

What's next for this artist of many talents? He is, after all, just 40 and, in some ways, still in the early stages of what should be a long career. Ironically, and perhaps appropriately, as this book went to press, Byrne and his young family were moving a short walk away from their SoHo loft to a townhouse in Greenwich Village. Perhaps a first chapter is finally drawing to a close.

But a prediction can only be paraphrased in Byrne terms. In the electronic soup of images and sounds in which we all try to live our lives, his future, as does ours, looks like more of the same...but, of course, different.

Any other hints will have to be construed from the conversation and sample work that follow.

ARTIST
IN DIALOGUE

JOHN HOWELL: You've said that you have often looked back at your various projects and found common threads running through all of them. How would you define the beginnings of that thread in Talking Heads music?

DAVID BYRNE: The pretty early Talking Heads stuff often had a strong rhythmic, funky underpinning. Europeans used to say it had elements of Booker T and the MGs and that Stax/Volt [*home of Sam and Dave, Isaac Hayes and Rufus Thomas—JH*] soul sound. That wasn't always apparent to Americans; maybe Americans are too close to that kind of music. There was always a pretty heavy black influence in what we were doing, more than in most punk music. So I guess there's a thread of taking various vernacular forms and playing around with them a little bit—whether it's slightly African stuff, or slightly Latin, or whether there are elements of zydeco in one song or blues in another. It's all stuff that you happen to live with. There are traces of the thread all through American pop music.

HOWELL: Which is a wildly impure music.

BYRNE: Yeah. And occasionally, like in the record I did with Brian Eno [*My Life in the Bush of Ghosts*], we threw Middle Eastern vocals or Middle Eastern melody lines on top, but most of the rhythmic underpinnings had more of an African influence. There are exceptions, but most of the stuff has elements that are found in American popular music. I can't get outside of that.

HOWELL: Another early thread for the band, which you've mentioned before, was a rejection of artifice.

BYRNE: Yeah, but a lot of that has crept back in. We also threw out drum and guitar solos, and visually we tried to throw out as much of the artifice as possible. There was a period when glitter-rock was popular, and everyone who got on-stage, even in little clubs, was getting all dressed up and doing all that kind of showy stuff. Talking Heads and some of the other groups felt like, "Why not just get up and play in street clothes?" And sometimes I'd take that idea further, as a conceptual idea, and say, "What is the average person in New York wearing on the street?" It would be a polyester suit or something. Nothing garish, just a cheap suit. Occasionally I'd try to perform in something like that, but it really wasn't very practical, so we sometimes ended up just looking like young, clean-cut Americans.

> *Talking Heads and some of the other groups felt like, 'Why not just get up and play in street clothes?'*

HOWELL: Young Republicans.

BYRNE: Yeah. The look wasn't real, but the idea—if one had to say what the idea was—might be something like that. If in some kind of bizarre world someone might say, "What does a young American look like?" it might look like that. What happened was that idea became an artifice in itself. You couldn't get rid of artifice by saying, "We'll look real average so that what matters is what we do. Our actions matter, and the music matters and our gestures matter. We're not communicating by our clothes." That ended up being a load of bullshit. You can't get away from it. Around 1979, when I was on the verge of admitting more irrational things into music and into what I was thinking, I also noticed that people who put on theatrical performances in the East—in Japan and Bali—just seemed to be doing it for themselves or for their community. They seemed to accept that you had to get dressed up if you were going to go onstage. You had to make yourself something bigger than life.

HOWELL: Otherwise it's almost insulting.

BYRNE: Yeah, if somebody goes on dressed in their street clothes, it's not really a show. Put the flowers out, put on the make-up, get the costumes out and all that kind of thing. I guess it takes getting away from home to see that there's a certain power to that. This artifice communicates on another level and helps you get stuff across in another way. Obviously being on-stage is not like sitting around chatting. It's an artificial situation to begin with.

HOWELL: So you had to invent a new way to be artificial?

BYRNE: Yes. That's when I started thinking of organizing what the group was wearing on-stage and doing stuff in videos that was obviously not a depiction of real life. We thought out what we wore and the degree to which our presentation was going to be stylized.

HOWELL: And that's when Talking Heads performances began to get larger-than-life, like with your oversize suit. By the *Stop Making Sense* tour, you looked as though you were being transported on-stage. In *Talking Heads vs. Television [1984 BBC footage shot in collaboration with the band, recut in 1989—JH]* there were many cross-references between music and shamanism. Explicit parallels were drawn between preachers, ministers, witch doctors, gurus, *griots* and what the Talking Heads were doing in music and movement. Was your persona as an Everyman-turned-seer planned or did it emerge in the process of performing?

BYRNE: A little bit of both. Some of the stuff developed as the performance went along; we'd notice that some of our movements, like suddenly putting hands up, were archetypal gestures. But in that video clip I did for *Once in a Lifetime*, for example, I watched a bunch of footage of preachers and people getting the spirit in churches, and I made a dance vocabulary out of that. Toni Basil, a choreographer I worked with, would look at it and say, "No, you've done that one before, do something else." She helped me put it into order. Once I got the rhythm of it, some of it would come spontaneously. It wasn't all predetermined. It was a mixture of being intellectual or predetermined or choreographic-intuitive. Which is, I suppose, the way a lot of people paint and write songs or whatever.

HOWELL: You've been characterized in most stories as shy and reserved, yet this seems at odds with your stage persona.

BYRNE: Inside I'm an outgoing egomaniac. But it only comes out, luckily, on-stage. It's a boring cliché that the stage persona compliments the day-to-day person. Let the psychobabblers work it out.

HOWELL: Do you ever get stage fright?

BYRNE: Yes and no. I've never been afraid to go on, but I always have to lighten my load—I shit and piss—before going on-stage. This is, I believe, a basic animal adrenaline reaction. A preparation for flight.

I also lose the ability to concentrate, to have a normal conversation.

HOWELL: About your stage persona—it's not unusual for artists to assume a spiritual sense, to take on some kind of prophetic tone. For pop musicians that has often meant the role of a cultural prophet, even a shamanistic voice.

BYRNE: Yes, I'm aware of that, and I didn't want to take on the role of being a prophet or shaman on-stage. That can turn into a caricature that gets hokey after a while. There may be elements of that, but I didn't want to set myself up as a prophet or anything like that. I just wanted to say that we are part of that and so are lots of other people. That's the nature of the beast if you're part of that tradition—almost whether you like it or not. When we listened to a lot of African, Latin and American funk music, one thing that was common to all of them was that the rhythms were syncopated, which means that there is more than one rhythm happening at once. The structure of the music was that the whole was greater than the sum of its parts and that each part was just a little piece—together they made something that was not evident in any one piece. What seemed wonderful about that idea was that it was a musical metaphor for a utopian community. Each part had its identity and fit together with the others to create something else—and they all benefitted by getting something in return. By giving their little bit, each musician partakes in an ecstatic feeling that results when all the parts are put together. When the band moved from a four-piece to a nine-piece group, it kind of validated that idea. It was maybe a little evident in the studio, but you didn't get the real visceral experience until it was fully formed. You could see all these things fit together, and you got this electric charge when everything jelled. When it didn't, it was a mess. But when it did you got this very communal spark which was different from the kind of feeling you get with other kinds of pop music.

HOWELL: A temporary transcendence of the ego?

BYRNE: Yeah.

HOWELL: When you mention a utopian community you seem to imply a vision of a world that is better than the one we're in now...

BYRNE: Yeah. And even if it's never possible socially, it's possible in a metaphorical way—musically or through other kinds of media. You

> *I didn't want to take on the role of being a prophet or shaman on-stage.*

Warming up for the tour at the Bardavon Theater in Poughkeepsie, New York.

41

can get a small taste of transcending individual egos.

HOWELL: What's so important about that particular feeling and idea?

BYRNE: Even if it's only for thirty seconds or so, you get a glimpse of everything in harmony and balance. It's very nice, and it's enough sometimes just to get a glimpse of it, a little taste of something that's greater than the shithole that we live in. There's a certain amount of satisfaction in that you don't always have to have this huge desire to open the whole door: It's enough to get a peek through the keyhole.

> *I used to work out some choreography by improvising at home.*

You can transcend for just a moment in some way that seems kind of sensual and spiritual but not in a fuzzy way—in a way that's real and gritty and sexy and everything like that.

HOWELL: You describe this as a feeling that happens in performance, but for a long while after *Stop Making Sense* you did not perform at all.

BYRNE: It happened a little when we were recording *Rei Momo* in the studio because there were a bunch of us recording at once.

HOWELL: Does it happen when you're directing a film? Transcendent is not the word is it? (Laughs.)

BYRNE: Not as much. In a funny way, it can happen when stuff is edited together. You start to look at one image next to another somewhat unrelated one, and sometimes they jump from one thing to another. You can be in two places at once or perceive two things simultaneously.

HOWELL: Do you like to dance socially?

BYRNE: Yes. But mostly to funk, *soukous*, salsa, Bomb Squad mixes, *forro*—if it's really fast—and a couple of twelve-inch mixes. Once in while in clubs, but never in discos. Most of the grooves don't swing enough for me. Maybe that's changing now—I've been busy.

HOWELL: Did any of your staged dance moves grow out of your private fooling around?

BYRNE: I used to work out some choreography by improvising at home. Some of the moves in *Stop Making Sense* were first improvised at home to dance tracks. I had Lynn Mabry and Ednah Holt *[the backing vocalists on the* Stop Making Sense *tour-JH]* improvise with me for a while at home. That was fun. I'd videotape it, like I used to do to my own improvisations, and then we'd look back and see if there was a moment that captured an energy or feeling or maybe looked cool from the audience's perspective. The rest was improvised in rehearsal or during the warm-up shows. Again I'd tape them on a home video system and look at them later in an attempt to remember the most inspired moments. The process is almost exactly like writing songs—choreography for musicians... Turns out it's the same process a lot of the street dancers use: improv, refine... improv, refine... Over and over until something organically falls into its most natural or surprising place. Toni Basil helped me see that this was what I was already doing when we did the "Once in a Lifetime" video together. At the same time I noticed the same process being used in some of the most surprising places. I could see that gospel preachers had

If I sit down to write a song and ask myself, 'What do I want to say?' I find it really difficult to do.

refined a sermon over many performances so that it would bridge into a song.... Jazz musicians's spontaneous improvisations grow out of years of practice.... I could see it in the most gut-wrenching and moving acts; the performances had been—sometimes unconsciously—worked over. This isn't cynical. It's a process that is built into our organism, a kind of learning curve.

HOWELL: When Talking Heads first started, did creating music in the conscious context of art—particularly conceptual art—ever make it stilted?

BYRNE: I don't know how to answer that exactly. If art is the church of the upper class and rock-and-roll is the church of the lower class, then what happens when they meet? Boom? Have the middle class and the bourgeoisie emulated the upper classes again? Are the crowds flooding the Met hoping for some kind of spiritual boon or blessing? Would they be better off at CBGB's? I don't know.

HOWELL: Speaking of blessings, what about your own religious background? Were you raised in a particular religion?

BYRNE: Not really. I think for a while I went to a Presbyterian Church, then my parents moved and I went to a Methodist Church up the road. My Mom is now a Quaker, but that was after I had gone away to college. The religion I was aware of was pretty much that British/Scottish Presbyterian stuff.

HOWELL: Do any features of that interest you at all now?

BYRNE: No. Maybe at some point I'll get back to being able to appreciate what's good about it, but at the moment a lot of it seems like a very repressive take on Christianity. Maybe that's kind of necessary for Northern people—Scandinavians or Scots. It might have something to do with the climate and the way they live.

HOWELL: You brought an unusual emphasis on logic and reason to the early Talking Heads songs—both in their taut arrangements and in the sometimes hyperrational lyrics. It seemed like you were approaching the pop song from a pretty oblique angle. Maybe you were even questioning the notion of a career in pop music.

BYRNE: We've grown up in the environment of pop songs. It certainly wasn't something new that we were creating. It was a given form. There wasn't any real excitement in just accepting it as is. But in a way, it was kind of neat to go into something that did have rules and boundaries. It seemed better that we didn't have total freedom, that there were rules to abide by. I guess that also applies to found footage. We grew up with all of that stuff. As they say in books and magazines, our environment is as much movies and television as it is birds and trees and other people.

HOWELL: Can you talk about how you write songs?

BYRNE: It seems to take a familiar path, no matter what the specific details are. Details such as words or music first, or riff versus melody, are aspects of a larger process. I see it as a process of regurgitation and then molding. The regurgitation of gut, unconscious, God-given or pure material is an intuitive, magical process. Then that mess of unformed yet powerful stuff is molded by art or craft into a song—or whatever it seems to want to be. The first part is not intellectual, the second part is equal parts intellect and craft, or skill. I think everyone from Hank Williams to John Cage probably goes through a similar, if not identical process, although, of course, many of the details would be different. And maybe the details are what makes each one unique. Like a strand of DNA.

HOWELL: You sometimes use narrating personae, like in "Psycho Killer." Does this make it easier to write?

BYRNE: If I sit down to write a song and ask myself, "What do I want to say?" I find it really difficult to do. But it's easy if I put myself in someone else's shoes and say, "What would this person feel strongly about?" It takes away the responsibility for my actions—somebody else can do it. In a lot of the songs on *Uh-Oh* I tried to really say something, or make them be about something, whereas some of my songs on the Talking Heads records, if you had asked me what the songs were about, I really couldn't tell you, even in retrospect. Lyrically, I've tried to get the imagery of each line or phrase to have a resonance to it, so it has a strength of its own.

HOWELL: Let me get some brief responses on some of the songs on *Uh-Oh*. "Now I'm Your Mom"?

BYRNE: That's a song about a sex change. A sensitive ditty about a man's decision to cut his dick off.

HOWELL: "Girls On My Mind"?

BYRNE: It's one of those stupid, truthful things that you kind of blurt out.

HOWELL: "Something Ain't Right"?

BYRNE: That was something I wrote with Terry Allen. I sent him an early track when we were first recording. I was improvising words, and he sent back some suggested verses. Some of the lines are his, some are mine. It's a rant against the Old Fart Upstairs.

HOWELL: "She's Mad"?

BYRNE: That's three minutes of domestic hell with a little bit of bliss thrown in.

HOWELL: "The Cowboy Mambo"?

BYRNE: I think each verse is about something different. The last verse, about the shithouse, I was real happy with. It was one of the truer statements I think I've written.

HOWELL: "Monkey Man"?

BYRNE: It's about a guy returning from the war and seeing the state the country's in. His analysis is that evolution at some point must have started to reverse itself. This is a dream I actually had.

HOWELL: "Somebody"?

BYRNE: To me this is a song about the effects of racism on a woman, but it can be taken any number of ways.

HOWELL: What was the first song you wrote and performed?

BYRNE: "Bald-Headed Woman," I think it was called. I must have been about fifteen. Never performed it. The next song I wrote was "Psycho Killer." Now, when I was fifteen, I did record a bunch of other things over the next few years in high school. Multitracked performances of feedback. Tape cut-up experiments. That is, I recorded lots of sounds onto tape, and then cut up the tape at random and spliced it back together without knowing what order the sounds were in. They were primitive, multitracked things with mul-

Byrne dancing during the video shoot for Rei Momo.

tiple performances at different tape speeds. I also made a version of The Turtles's "Happy Together" with Tupperware tubs for drums. I'm more conservative now, huh?

HOWELL: You spent two years in school—at the Rhode Island School of Design and at the Maryland Institute College of Art. How do you think formal education affects the creative process?

BYRNE: School is an expensive way to meet like-minded individuals one's own age. One might, if lucky, come upon one or two real teachers who are inspirational. That's all we can expect.

> *School is an expensive way to meet like-minded individuals one's own age.*

HOWELL: How about the role of art and music criticism in the creative process?

BYRNE: There's no simple way to look at criticism. Is the critic a *Consumer Reports* for the public? A buyer beware? A mirror for the artist? A leech living off the creativity of others? A handmaid to the record industry? A thing to fill space in between advertisements? Are they the philosophers of cool? Are they naming the unnameable? Are they failed musicians getting revenge? They are all of the above.

HOWELL: There is a period in your career that I'm unclear about. After you stopped going to school and before you moved back to Rhode Island, what did you do with yourself?

BYRNE: I dropped out, bummed around the country, stayed on a hippie commune, formed a duo called Bizadi with a friend who played accordion. I played ukulele and violin—we did old standards. I also made some videotapes.

HOWELL: You've said that you were involved in conceptual art when you went to art school and lived in Providence. You were interested in lists and art that was more verbally than visually oriented. How did that color your approach to music?

BYRNE: Well, I guess a lot of people feel that if they're going to make something, the first thing to do is to throw out everything you know or everything that's given and start from scratch. And in a way that seemed true about that kind of art. Throw away all the paintings and art becomes a manifestation of an idea. So why not just write down the idea? A lot of pop music with its guitar and drum solos seemed to be superfluous to the idea of what the music was about. So why not strip it down and deal with the idea, which often seemed to be textural rather than narrative? A lot of pop music communicated by texture rather than what the words were saying.

HOWELL: But your use of African and Latin music has led you to the extreme end of the continuum.

BYRNE: Yeah.

HOWELL: You're adding texture beyond belief. The more confusing the elements, the more interesting it gets. The ideas in your music aren't as logical, as language oriented. They're rhythmic ideas maybe.

BYRNE: Yeah. If you did just one pop song with pounding drums and rhythms, you'd say, "Oh, that's using the idea of African music." But when you get beyond that, the ideas and rhythms are more complicated. I guess I'm not dealing with the same thing anymore. I'm not dealing so much with art or music as an intellectual idea so much as admitting a lot of stuff that's irrational or intuitive, where this is no longer just a pure idea. Instead this is a pure musical idea.

HOWELL: When did this shift toward the irrational occur in your thinking?

BYRNE: Around 1979, I started listening to African music in a different way. I wasn't listening to it so much as a textural idea. I saw it as a whole different way of organizing and perceiving music, and that led me to the spirituality that created it in the first place.

HOWELL: Is that also what interested you about the Bahian dances? [*In 1989, Byrne filmed,* Ilé Aiyé (The House of Life), *a documentary about the Candomblé Nago religion of Bahia in northern Brazil.—JH*]

BYRNE: Yes, it's the same tradition.

HOWELL: The transcendent qualities of music seem more real there. It seems that people live it somewhat more.

BYRNE: They do live it more. It's much more in the foreground. I was listening to the music over and over again before I went to Bahia the first time. I wanted to go there because I thought there was something underlying this music that enables people to do stuff that I think is great and that I want to know about. The film [*Ilé Aiyé*] was searching for a little bit of that, in a way. I wanted to find out what that kind of spirituality or sensibility was. That sensibility pervades certain parts of Brazil, but not everywhere.

HOWELL: Do you see the Candomblé rituals as shows—live performances—in the same sense that yours are?

BYRNE: Someone who wrote about the Candomblé stuff in Brazil in the past described it as a show. I guess in one sense you could say that a church service is a show—a theatrical ritual with costumes and stag-

© F-STOP FITZGERALD

Byrne as the front man for Talking Heads, shows a hint of that "Young Republican" look.

ing and all that kind of thing—and that in one sense the secular show shares elements with the sacred show. But there are a bunch of differences. The way the audience apprehends it is different...

HOWELL: Going on the road to support a new record is usually just part of the machinery of rock-and-roll. But these Candomblé rituals, for example, have a different logic behind them. Possession, spirits loose in the theater—you don't just order those up for a show. Has music embedded in different cultures changed the way you think about your own performances?

BYRNE: Well, I suppose each time you go on-stage it's a good idea to stop and ask yourself, "What are we doing this for? Why are we we going on-stage? What kind of music is this? What does it mean when you ask this question?" Really throw them out. If those questions are hovering out there, then the answers to the small questions like what kind of costumes you should wear will make more sense. They'll have some relationship to the bigger questions like: Why make a performance? Why is a theatrical thing a kind of ritual, and what kind of ritual is it? What's the relationship to the audience? What do I get out of it and what do you get out of it? It's not very easy to find answers, but it's nice to have the questions hovering around.

HOWELL: By the end of the *Stop Making Sense* tour these questions seemed to have been played out for Talking Heads. Is that why you never toured the songs from the last several Heads albums?

BYRNE: Yes. There has to be a reason for doing it. Not necessarily a clear, obvious reason, but at least a subliminal reason.

HOWELL: At this point, you've released several anthologies of Latin music on Luaka Bop, directed the Bahia documentary and recorded an album of original Latin-flavored songs, *Rei Momo*. But when you were first exploring Brazilian music you said you had to buy records blind or because you liked their covers...

BYRNE: Yeah. What else do you have to go on most of the time? Now that there's this kind of world music explosion, or mini-explosion, there's a lot more information available—published lists of the pick hits and lists of artists from different countries. There's a book out now that gives a history of African pop music starting from the fifties. Now you don't have to be quite as blind to find that music in this country—but it was kind of fun anyway. I loved these cultural hybrids, when an album cover would have a drawing of a car with seventeen headlights on it, and I thought, "What is this?" It was obviously a mixture of American and other cultures, and I thought it was pretty great. Something new was coming out of it. I already had a bunch of ethnic field recordings—and that's great as far as it goes—but there's something vital and alive when a new hybrid emerges.

HOWELL: But aren't you still coming out of the context of an American music culture that's based on these hybrids?

BYRNE: Yeah. Rock-and-roll comes from rhythm and blues, gospel, and country and western—which, in turn, comes from African music, Celtic music and European bardic songs and so on. We grew up listening to a musical mishmash. Even in the short life of American popular music that I've been witness to, I've noticed all sorts of elements

The Beatles included at least one cha-cha on each of their early records.

coming in and out of rock-and-roll. There was a period when they were doing lots of cha-chas. The Beatles included at least one cha-cha on each of their early records. You don't see bands doing that too much anymore.

HOWELL: Appropriating the music is easy enough. You can borrow a rhythm or pick up a phrase or an instrument. But the real subject of the film, *Ilé Aiyé*, is the spirituality and the state of mind....

BYRNE: I don't think you can appropriate a sensibility wholesale. You can't really transplant it. I think someone foreign can only absorb it on their own terms. You might be able to approach the way someone else feels about it, but you'll never quite get it in the same way. It's like, say, the Hare Krishnas; there's a valid idea there and a valid spiritual concept and something quite deep. But somehow the robes and haircuts and rituals—the manifestations of the deeper spirituality throughout Indian culture—aren't relevant when transplanted to Western culture. The details should be changed. Playing Indian music on the streets of New York in white robes doesn't make any sense.

HOWELL: The details supersede everything else. It's like watching a show.

BYRNE: The details don't have any relevance to our culture or background. They need to be reinvented or rejuvenated, whatever that means. Using Walkmen or ghetto blasters... I don't know what the new terms would be, but I think it sometimes happens, in the way that youth get a taste of energy from rock concerts that they don't get anywhere else.

Byrne concentrating on a solo.

HOWELL: That kind of energy is also present in some churches here in the states. When I was growing up in the South I went to my maid's church sometimes. Having been raised as a Southern Presbyterian—a devotee of Calvin—I couldn't believe the minister wore a guitar. He'd preach about Jonah and the whale, and he'd hit heavy-metal chords with the word "whale." I thought it was too much fun, too exciting to possibly be church. But Southern churches are built around music—both black ones and fundamentalist white ones, like the kind Jerry Lee Lewis grew up in. It's a spiritual culture that uses music.

BYRNE: That kind of energy wasn't present in the churches I went to. When you went to those Baptist churches, you were aware that there was another kind of energy, even if you denied that it was spiritual. You can call it whatever you like, but you were aware that there was some kind of thing that was going on. Sometimes it gets translated into popular culture in new forms, and certain aspects of it survive and become high-tech and modern. In an ideal world, some of the deeper spirituality would be imparted through popular films. And in an ideal world, there would be a sacred manifestation of secular music and spirit as well.

HOWELL: When you began to hear Brazilian music, did the Bahian influence—the more African elements—stand out to you?

BYRNE: Not in a hard-cut way, but yeah. You could say in this country, for instance, that a lot of rock-and-roll comes from the Memphis/New Orleans axis, that part of the country. It may be not quite as true today; but in Brazil it's still true that Bahia is a wellspring of creativity, and a lot of other parts of the country sort of polish it up. I was aware of that, a little bit.

HOWELL: Why is Bahia such a focal point?

BYRNE: People mythologized Bahia. It would get quoted in songs. It started to pick up a mythic aura of being the place where all this music was emanating from. Without even knowing why, you were picking up undercurrents from stuff that you heard or read. So when Fabiano Canosa from the Public Theatre invited *True Stories* to be in the Rio Film Festival in December of '87, I knew enough to go to Bahia first for ten days. It was a shock.

HOWELL: Was it as much like going to Africa as it was going to Brazil?

BYRNE: Yeah, I guess so.

HOWELL: Are the people there from the same Western African population that was brought to North America and the Caribbean?

Brazilian Music

BYRNE: Yeah, there are slight variations. Some parts would be more heavily Yoruba, some more Fon, and some more from the Congo region, depending on the route of the slave ships. The Portuguese were among the big slave traders; they had slave ports in Angola, where they still speak Portuguese. So a lot of African influence in Bahia came from Angola... But the rhythms that came out of different places were culturally slightly different. In Bahia there are two kinds of Candomblé. There's what they call Nago, which is more Yoruba-derived, and then there's Angolic, which is more Angola-derived. They have more the same pantheon of gods. The dances have minor differences. The rhythms are slightly different, but they mix them together all the time depending on what the drummer feels like playing. Trying to keep it straight and be academic about it gets kind of pointless after a while.

HOWELL: What was Arto Lindsay's involvement with *Beleza Tropical* [*Byrne's first compilation of Brazilian music, released in 1989—JH*]?

BYRNE: I approached him about doing three things: liner notes, translation, and input on selections so that I'd get a quick crash course on what this music was about.

HOWELL: So he was a consultant?

BYRNE: Yeah, kind of. He told me about the *Tropicalismo* movement.

HOWELL: Tell me about your first reaction to Brazilian music.

BYRNE: More than ten years ago Island came out with a few Jorge Ben records. In fact, one of those songs, "Caramba!" is on *Beleza Tropical*. Later I bought a live Milton Nascimento record. The Jorge Ben sounded too laid back for my taste at the time, and Milton's voice sounded almost too operatic, just letting it all out in this high voice. I thought, "I don't get this."

HOWELL: So now that you've become more laid back and operatic yourself, it sounds just right.

BYRNE: Yes.

HOWELL: Did you remix or remaster the songs for *Beleza Tropical*?

BYRNE: We remastered them all. We got digital transfers of all the originals. We slightly recued the masters, but we didn't remix anything. The technology has come a long way since those songs were pressed in Brazilian plastic. So they sound more hi-fi, more contemporary than on the records I originally heard. It's kind of nice.

HOWELL: You were criticized for the song selection on *Beleza Tropical*. How did you make those decisions? Did you decide to leave somebody off the record and later feel you had made a mistake?

BYRNE: Yeah, there was some stuff that got left off and I thought, "I know this person is very popular; they're actually of the same period, and it should be in there." But I personally didn't like their stuff as much, so what can I do? I wasn't attempting to make a democratic selection.

HOWELL: I suppose there's the feeling that for a scholarly, or more musicological project, you would have to have been more judicious and included cuts that represented something, even if you didn't care for them personally.

BYRNE: Yeah, if it had been put out by the Smithsonian or a record label that had the pretense of being scholarly.

HOWELL: I remember I was at this reading for, I think, Greil Marcus's *Lipstick Traces*, and someone popped up and asked the inevitable question: "Why is this so white Eurocentric?"

BYRNE: You mean the Sex Pistols thing? I think we have this romantic notion that Third World music has more of the pure essence than our corrupt, commercialized music, that it's more spiritual—not in the sense that they're singing about God, but in the sense that it comes more from the spirit. There is sometimes a bit of truth to that, and sometimes it's a lot of hogwash. I think the exact same thing applies to the Sex Pistols; they were a totally bogus romantic thing as well. They're something that was put together by Malcolm McLaren, and people fell for it hook, line, and sinker. To me it was like, once again, here comes the rock-and-roll image of bad boys in black leather. It used to be bad boys in drag, and now it's bad boys in ripped clothing. It's just another romantic notion that Europeans like to go for: the drunk on the corner has more wisdom than the guy in the ivory tower.

HOWELL: Many artists have traveled to other continents—places they see as primitive and, therefore, somehow more authentic—and incorporated the native art forms into their own work. Some people see it as a rip-off; some read it as a gesture against the artificiality of industrial society. Either way, have you bought into that pretense?

BYRNE: I don't know how to deal with that. I can't deny that I'm guilty of part of that, or that I'm susceptible to it. But, at the same time, I think a lot of it doesn't matter.

HOWELL: Perhaps it's a question of who it matters to.

BYRNE: It depends on what you take from Third World cultures, if you're just a plunderer. I would hope that there are some ethics involved. I guess the reason people think it's a problem is because we make more money off of it. That's where the difference lies, in the economics of it.

HOWELL: Looking at the popularity of *Beleza Tropical*, I'm sure the musicians on it are not unhappy. I'm sure they're getting some money.

BYRNE: Yeah. Not that they need it. Most of them are pretty big stars. Not all of them, but most of them are doing pretty well financially. They don't mind selling a few more records.

HOWELL: Nevertheless, the film and the records raise the question of whether or not it's possible, or perhaps, justifiable, to stray that far from your roots.

BYRNE: The bias I feel I'm most guilty of is the desire for Brazilian or African or any Third World music to maintain a certain amount of cultural identity—whatever that is. When Gilberto Gil, for instance, does a lot of reggae songs, just straight, rock-guitar reggae...

HOWELL: ...rock steady...

BYRNE: They're good songs, well done, with wonderful political lyrics, but at the same time, why do I want to hear a Brazilian play reggae? A lot of Africans play reggae and I don't care how good it is, I'll never get over the idea that I want to hear Jamaicans play reggae. From Brazilians I want to hear something that sounds uniquely Brazilian. I don't want to hear them playing rock-and-roll, either, which a lot of them now play. Heavy metal is getting very popular in Brazil. It's

The old Celia Cruz recordings and some other kinds of Latin music are all I've been listening to for the last few years.

our cultural bias that we're saying, "No, you shouldn't do that; you should do your own thing." We have no right to say that. Why shouldn't they play reggae or heavy metal or rock-and-roll? They have as much right to do that as we do to incorporate Brazilian elements into our music. It's like me, putting in African or Brazilian elements into stuff I do. Actually, people could say, "Well, that's very nice, but you should stick to rock-and-roll."

HOWELL: People did say that about some of the records.

BYRNE: Yeah. Brazilians said, "You shouldn't try to do Brazilian stuff. You should do rock-and-roll, you do it really good. There are plenty of good Latin groups all over the place. Why do you need to turn into another one?"

HOWELL: This brings up a point your critics seem to be ignoring: How

Byrne takes a pause during the shooting of the Rei Momo video.

can you ask someone to be blind to other cultures?

BYRNE: Yeah. In truth, the old Celia Cruz recordings and some other kinds of Latin music are all I've been listening to for the last few years. Yet I'm supposed to segregate it and say, "I can enjoy this, but I really should be playing something else." I can't do that. I really find a lot of beauty in the religion and spirituality, and there's something there that seems contemporary. Granted, I'm kind of taking it on my own terms, but there's something there that speaks to a more contemporary sensibility. I'm not going to toss it away. I'm going to say: "Here it is. This is something great. It's joyous and interesting."

HOWELL: How did you pick the musicians for *Rei Momo*?

BYRNE: Most of them I didn't pick. I got in touch with a recording engineer who has recorded a lot of Latin acts. I met with him and a percussionist a couple times and talked about what kind of musicians would be appropriate, which is kind of what we did with the African musicians in Paris as well [for Talking Heads's album *Naked*]. We had a go-between, somebody who would bring in musicians and get to know them and try things out.

HOWELL: How did you describe to the Latin musicians what you wanted?

BYRNE: I'd play them tapes I'd done. They'd say, "Oh, that sounds like merengue." Then I'd say, "Oh good, it was intended to sound like merengue." And we would talk about it; I'd say, "I'd really like to use traditional merengue instrumentation," and they'd say, "You need this." Or I'd say, "I would like to change this." For instance, there's an old Cuban/Latin style called *charanga*, pre-Fidel—after Fidel too—but it's not as popular as salsa now. It usually has a very shrill kind of flute improvising on top, with the voice just floating somewhere in between the flute and the violins. I've never gotten used to that flute on top, so I said I'd like to do it without the flute, using just violins playing sweet rhythmic lines. So I kind of messed with it a little bit. It's very interesting for me to see how many rules there are. There are usually at least three percussionists. If you say you're doing a certain kind of song, each of the percussionists knows what to do. When they get to a particular section, the song will have a chorus section and the bongo player will put down his bongos and pick up a bell and start playing a bell part. He knows what kind of part to play. You don't need to tell them what to do; they already know exactly what to do. It's great. If you say the rhythm of a particular song is *montuno*, that tells you what each person plays, the kind of lines the piano player plays. If you want, it tells you what kind of brass parts there are and if the song is romantic or not. All these parameters are set out for you, which is kind of nice. Steve Lillywhite, the producer of the album, pointed out that you can look at it as restricting but that it's also great because the different parts have been tried and tested so everybody knows that it's going to work. But then, of course, we mess with it later on down the line, throwing it a little off-kilter, so it's not all traditional.

HOWELL: How did the creative process work? Who ended up composing the music?

BYRNE: Well, I met them more than halfway. I'd write a song with a specific Latin rhythm in mind, play it on guitar, and their group would play it. It would be fairly straightforward. They would do it in their style because that was the way it was intended. Then I'd fuck with it from there. I'd say, "That sounds good, but let's change this and move a little bit from being quite so traditional." They loved that, and we'd see how far we could bend it before the rhythm began not to swing anymore.

HOWELL: It's not very traditional for a Latin chorus to sing, "I'm elegant," and then turn around and sing, "but I'm also pathetic."

BYRNE: I threw in lyrics and melodies that are not very Latin. Sometimes the melodies were typical, but often they were more like melodies that I would write for Talking Heads. They're done to those rhythms, though. The melodies and lyrics are layered on top. Of course, my lyrics are nothing like the typical lyrics for Latin songs, but then neither are Rubén Blades's or Willie Colón's lyrics. They've broken out of the mold of typical Latin lyrics.

HOWELL: Do you see this synthesis of Latin tradition and your ideas as creating a third kind of music?

BYRNE: It might be. Every once in a while I think we get that. Not on every tune, not on everything we've been working on; but maybe ten percent of the time, there might be something new. The rest is layering. It might be successful musically or lyrically, but you're still aware of the layering. You might feel that they haven't quite meshed together. Occasionally we'll get something completely new out of it, where the seams aren't visible at all. Not that the goal is to perform some kind of trick. But it is neat when that happens, and you don't know what it is anymore. I saw an interview with Ray Barretto on television. They were asking about the song we did for *Something Wild* ["Loco De Amor"] because in Latin news there's always talk about the big crossover. When is Latin music going to cross over? Most of the musicians of his generation aren't interested in that anymore. They could give a fuck because they have already been that route. People said that if they compromised their music a little bit here and there they might appeal more to a rock audience and mainstream America would love them. I guess he did some of that in the early sixties and he looks back on those records now as being silly.

HOWELL: Disco?

BYRNE: No, they were Latin boogaloo. Some of them were pretty good, but some of them were really silly. But then Barretto renounced it and went back to Latin stuff. Anyway, they asked him about the stuff that we did, and he said it worked because I didn't ask the musicians to play rock music.

Lyrically or imagistically or musically, it's most exciting when you can't quite get a handle on it.

Neither was I coming in and saying, "You do what you do, and I'm just going to jump on top of it." It was a mixture—something in between.

HOWELL: Why do you think it's so important to make something that we don't know what it is? Is that what you're interested in most?

BYRNE: Yes. Lyrically or imagistically or musically, it's most exciting when you can't quite get a handle on it.

HOWELL: Why do you think we have this constant impulse to get to that place where that new music takes us?

BYRNE: It frees your mind, or frees your body up for an instant when you don't know what's happening, when your mooring has been cut or your perception has been loosened. You don't have the music already pegged for what it is. It throws you for a while. For an instant, you reorder the way you look at things or the way you feel until you create a new word for the experience.

HOWELL: You talked about losing yourself while you're performing. Another way to lose yourself in something is to have it so spelled out and defined that the intensity you spend on execution tunnels through to another place.

BYRNE: That's true with a lot of this Latin music. Within traditional styles, there are rules about everything. It's all given. Everybody slips right into it.

HOWELL: So that frees you up to allow something else to happen.

BYRNE: Yeah, your mind isn't occupied with doing that part of it, so you can do something else.

HOWELL: In *True Stories* you intercut several parallel story lines. At one point you said you'd written a draft of the script and there was not enough story. And then Beth Henley worked on it, and you thought there was too much story. But when you finally did it, you thought there was just the right amount of story.

> *I always thought that it was possible to have a thread that wasn't a conventional narrative.*

BYRNE: I always thought that it was possible to have a thread through something that wasn't a conventional narrative.

HOWELL: What is a conventional narrative to you?

BYRNE: Well, in a movie you introduce the characters in the first act, and there's a love triangle—a man and two women or a woman and two men or six women and three men...

HOWELL: Two triangles. (Laughs.) That's conventional, all right.

BYRNE: ... And there's a conflict in motion, and it plays out in the second act and gets resolved in the third. Everything you see or hear works to push that story forward. Not much is peripheral. There's always something geared to moving the motor of the narrative.

HOWELL: The narrative engine.

BYRNE: Yeah. And once that narrative engine is set in motion, everything has to keep it running.

HOWELL: What's lost when that happens?

BYRNE: It seems like you're looking at life with blinders on. When it works, it's like you're experiencing a contemporary vision of an old myth. It has a lot of power when something in the story strikes a rhythm or chord, when it means something to you. But when it doesn't, when it's just a bunch of cops chasing after a bag of cocaine, it may keep your interest but it seems like a kind of fascist way of looking at life. Anything that's peripheral to this story gets shoved out. I don't think there's anything wrong with seeing the figure manipulating the puppets—the Wizard of Oz behind the screen. But when you constantly have the sense that *you're* the puppet and this thing is dragging you along, it's an unpleasant feeling.

HOWELL: Is that why you stepped into *True Stories?* You were directing it and also acting in it as if to say, "Here's the puppeteer?"

A complete selection of backstage passes for the Rei Momo tour.

BYRNE: Sort of. To be honest, I don't know if it was an entirely good idea for me to be in it. I directed, co-wrote, and did the music, so I didn't have to perform in it as well. It's the kind of thing that makes my ego seem too big. But from the practical side it probably helped to get it financed. In the end that was probably why I did it—to get the money and to get it done.

HOWELL: What was the budget for *True Stories*?

BYRNE: That was between two and three million.

HOWELL: Your character, the narrator, acts very wide-eyed on screen, as if he'd never seen what's going on before. Sort of a modern-day Candide. Was that difficult to do?

BYRNE: It's a fun way to be. I guess I'm a little bit like that, so I didn't feel I was really acting that much.

HOWELL: Your narrator is reminiscent of the narrator in Thornton Wilder's *Our Town*. Did you study that role?

BYRNE: When the movie script was in its third draft, someone said I should really read it before I went much further, so I did. And I watched the movie, too. I liked it a lot, though it was sentimental. As the narrator, I tried to recede to let the other characters come forward.

HOWELL: You've described *True Stories* as a hybrid of MTV and a Broadway musical. Is this a new movie-musical form?

BYRNE: I'm still not sure how this movie fits in. I tried to have the music come organically out of the scenes, and to put it in various musical styles that seem indigenous to where the scenes take place. At least when you see a song performed, it's in the style of music you would see in that place—from gospel country to a shopping-mall ballad...

HOWELL: ... A form you've revisited on your newest album [*Uh-Oh*]...

BYRNE: Yes. The song "Hanging Upside Down" is about mall rats. Manhattan and some of the areas around Manhattan are probably the only places where mall culture isn't so prevalent. It seems that in the whole rest of the country, that's where everyone goes to hang out.

HOWELL: What do you think of *True Stories* now, in terms of the balance between narrative and the peripheral events and images?

BYRNE: For some audiences I could probably have left in some of the little scenes that were cut out. But I didn't want it to be boring; I wanted it to keep zipping along. I'd seen other films where something pulls you through it, but it isn't a story that pulls you, it's something else.

HOWELL: One way you did that in *True Stories* was by having several stories.

BYRNE: Yeah, there were a few of them. Like in *Nashville,* where there were a few stories going at once and occasionally they'd cross each other. Sometimes the momentum that is generated in one scene overlaps into another and carries you through; you never stop to question how you got to this other place. You don't ask, "Why are we seeing this now? How does this relate to what we just saw a minute ago?" In a sense, you get the feeling that it's more realistic, like song lyrics that jump around and throw in words or phrases that are nonsequiturs. You're dealing with little bits of feelings and impulses and impressions that are jumbled up in the mind, rather than putting them into a rigidly defined narrative hierarchy. Maybe that is closer to the way things are actually perceived or felt. Sometimes it works. Something gets communicated, even though it's hard to specify what the words are about.

HOWELL: You've referred to two very different sources for *True Stories*: theater director Robert Wilson and the *Weekly World News* tabloid. How did those two influences come together for you?

BYRNE: I never thought about why the two together. That's a tough one. (Laughs.) Well, the *Weekly World News* tends to have stories that aren't really news, just odd stories. Some of the characters in the film were inspired by these articles.

HOWELL: Are the people in the paper real?

BYRNE: We didn't really ask if they'd made stuff up or not. Occasionally, the *News* would volunteer information like, "We don't know if you can say that; that's a real person." Which is a kind of backward admission that maybe some of their articles aren't based on real people.

HOWELL: How did Wilson's theater influence this raw material?

BYRNE: I've seen the way he works, and the way the Mabou Mines theater and the Wooster Group work too, and there's a general cut-and-paste construction method in their theater pieces, a lot of elements cut and pasted together to serve an overall structure rather than a story, like conventional theater work. That's the way I write songs—collect a lot of stuff, then put it into verses and choruses. I felt at home working that way.

HOWELL: You've said that you hoped *True Stories* would encourage people to look at things in their backyards with more respect. But some people criticized the movie's tone, saying it was condescending.

BYRNE: I certainly didn't feel that I was being condescending. And I don't think that the people we were filming felt that I was being condescending. They knew that some of the stuff we were doing was kind of ridiculous, like the men driving around in their little cars. That was obviously not serious; it was just for fun. I looked at it in that spirit. And because I kind of distanced myself from it—coming from downtown New York—I'd look at these minimal metal warehouses all over the place and think, "This is beautiful; this is the form-follows-function aesthetic carried through; this is economy of means." Philip Johnson and Mies van der Rohe and all these people have failed. Without even knowing about all of that verbiage and bullshit, those people in Texas succeeded in actually doing it—and occasionally it looked really beautiful. When those structures were plunked down on the flat Texas landscape, they looked like pieces of art stuck on a plinth or isolated in the white space of a gallery. They seemed to be in a big void. The ground was totally flat, and there was a big sky.

HOWELL: Some people may have had trouble believing that you meant that.

BYRNE: Yeah, they thought I was laughing up my sleeve, that I didn't believe those metal buildings were beautiful or that the shopping mall was great. A lot of people who saw the movie have a built-in bias against suburbia and middle-class America. Europeans are more willing to see a kind of naive creativity within middle-class Americans; they are more willing to accept that as a genuine creativity. They are more willing than sophisticated New Yorkers are to see it as something amazing and new. I also think that sometimes they just see it as bizarre... But they also see it as being something new and refreshing that gets rid of the baggage of European culture and creates something that's new without any preconceptions. It's a very idealistic way of looking at shopping malls and highways—and not without some elements of truth.

It's a very idealistic way of looking at shopping malls and highways—and not without some elements of truth.

HOWELL: Do you have any film projects lined up for the future?

BYRNE: Every couple of years I make the rounds with at least one new idea for a feature film I'd like to direct. So far, no one has reached into their pocket. Maybe I'll have to do like I did on *True Stories* and

put up the development money myself, so I don't have to go to these endless rounds of meetings. So, to answer, there is nothing to talk about as far as film is concerned today.

HOWELL: You've said that you want to discover the drama in ordinary things. Does that explain your use of found footage and shots of found objects—the history lessons and the town landscapes in *True Stories*, the archival, anthropological footage in *Talking Heads vs. Television*?

BYRNE: I like that type of footage on the level that it sort of widens the movie out, takes it out of the sphere of just dealing with certain people or a certain relationship. Plus, stock footage and bits and pieces of found stuff bring in other times and places just by virtue of the texture. You can throw in other references and put the story through a prism or kaleidoscope.

HOWELL: Remember the classic book everybody was reading in the sixties, *Man and His Symbols* [Carl Jung]? On one page you'd see an East Tennessee snake handler, on the next a witch doctor holding a snake in his hand.

BYRNE: Yeah. It's great to do that in film or video, because you get a real visceral sense of it.

HOWELL: Have you investigated any of that cross-cultural mythology in a systematic way?

BYRNE: Yeah, I've read a lot of Jung's books. I'm still plowing through some of them. I've read some of Joseph Campbell's books, too. He's kind of the Bob Thompson [*Robert Ferris Thompson, author of* Flash of the Spirit, *a study of African and Afro-American art and philosophy—JH*] of mythology. He can just run it off the top of his head.

HOWELL: And it all makes sense; it all fits. Some people may feel that it's surface culture-mongering, that as you develop a deeper understanding of different cultures you realize that you can't match them up just because a certain witch doctor has something in common with Ernest Angley [a televangelist], who is definitely a product of advanced Western capitalism.

BYRNE: But I like a lot of it. For me, it put things in perspective.

HOWELL: How so?

BYRNE: Well, by perspective, I mean that I can look at a movie or something and see how the various archetypes are being used. I can see that it is an old story being retold with cops and robbers instead of Samson and Delilah. When it works, it's nice, because you see that

this thing keeps happening over and over again. It tells you that there
is some order in the chaos of the universe. It's nice to think that
there's some sort of order, not just endless scribbling.

HOWELL: In the book about the making of *True Stories*, you gave credit to several still photographers' work as a visual inspiration to you.
Most filmmakers credit other filmmakers.

BYRNE: I guess that was because to some extent I'm still carrying over
a great deal of the way of doing things where the film is a series of
stills or stage pictures with things moving within the frame. So I
would look at other people's photos, and my own, almost like a stage
set or a frame that something could happen in. And then I'd think
of what would happen if you looked at this one and then that one
after this one, and then this one after that one, and so forth—a series
of drawings or photographs. It's not as true in this documentary, *Ilé
Aiyé*, the documentary set in Bahia, because you can't control things
as much, but there are elements snuck in there, almost like a still
photograph where something happens—a stone spins around, feath-
ers fall from the frame, or something like that. Iconic things outside
of the real world, or real world stuff filmed in a way that makes it
look iconic.

HOWELL: Why is that iconic sense so important to you?

BYRNE: It makes what you're seeing simultaneously real and a metaphor
for an idea. It distances it so that you know that it's real, that it's happening in front of a camera. At the same time, it can make it work
on another level too.

HOWELL: What is the value of the metaphor?

BYRNE: Telling two stories at once. You're telling a story on a deeper
level that may be unconscious, or maybe it's obvious, and then you're
telling a story that can be immediately perceived. I think people intu-
itively perceive both simultaneously. They may have problems when
they stop to intellectualize it, but when they're watching they can
perceive things two ways at once: what's in front of them and what's
behind it.

HOWELL: So intellectualization is a kind of static interference?

BYRNE: If by doing only that you can easily lose one whole level of meaning or one whole level of perceiving.

HOWELL: When you were filming *True Stories*, did you ever have trouble capturing an image?

BYRNE: Occasionally we couldn't get the right camera angle; we couldn't shoot something in the way that made it work like we wanted. Sometimes we'd find a way to make it work a little bit but not in the way we had imagined.

HOWELL: How did that work for videos? They operate under severe time constraints—two or three days.

BYRNE: Yeah, I discovered early on that there were unwritten rules. One was that the singer or performer had to be in it most of the time. Also, it generally has to be fairly fast-paced, the kind of thing that you can watch over and over again. The music really has to be at the forefront. Occasionally people get away with exceptions to that; but in most cases it can't be done like a film, where people are talking or having a fight or making love and the music is like a radio playing in the background. The music has to be really right there in front.

HOWELL: How does video figure into the pop success equation? You've always been very involved in making your videos, but are unestablished musicians susceptible to having their images manipulated?

BYRNE: We don't let our mamas dress us anymore, so why should we let someone else control the way we look on TV? No one should do a video that they don't believe in. Better they don't do any at all. I love them, but I'm perverted that way.

HOWELL: Which of the music videos you've made has been most satisfying or worked best for you, apart from all those rules?

BYRNE: I don't think there's a specific one; each of them is different from the other. Sometimes it was a fun challenge to work within those confines, and sometimes it got to be a drag, like, "Ah, here we go again; got to figure a new way of getting around this stuff."

HOWELL: In the film work that you have participated in—whether it's been as a subject in *Stop Making Sense* or a director in *True Stories* or the Bahia documentary—is there a certain look?

BYRNE: I'm not totally aware of it yet. It's probably there, but I don't know it. If it's there and it gets too strong, then I would be kind of scared and want to get away from it.

HOWELL: Scared of what?

BYRNE: That I was getting into a rut. Repeating myself.

HOWELL: There seems to be a contradiction in your earlier interest in anti-visual, conceptual, and language-based art and the wide variety of visual mediums you've ended up exploring.

BYRNE: When I was in school—and for a little while after that—doing non-visual things like questionnaires and lists, I would occasionally

Byrne directing the video shoot for Rei Momo.

do videos as well. I occasionally did stuff with Portapaks, those half-inch black-and-white video cameras. It was more idea-oriented than specifically visual, which was okay with that kind of equipment because the images weren't very rich and sensual. So it seemed kind of appropriate for that period and that kind of art. When I started doing pop videos, I was picking up a thread of that earlier work a little bit; there were elements of performance in them, but the cameras didn't move a whole bunch, or if they moved, they moved in a very stilted, formal way. The Portapak videos had a lot in common with art films at that time, in that there'd be a framework that was almost like a series of still pictures or tableaux. In the case of pop videos, they changed very quickly from one to the other. In a sense, each of those tableaux was a visual idea. They gradually got more and more pretty to look at, but I tried to keep them bare bones for the most part.

> *The ideal would be to have a tree in the middle of a landscape with nothing else around.*

HOWELL: What do you mean by bare bones?

BYRNE: I mean that if there was an image of a tree, the ideal would be to have a tree in the middle of a landscape with nothing else around. No houses, no fences, no mountains. Just a tree.

HOWELL: I have just gotten a glimpse of various boxes of your photographs. There are several different kinds of things there. Images of rocks, mental landscapes...another seemed to be a series of pictures looking up at light fixtures. Have you applied yourself to this with different interests at different times?

BYRNE: Yeah. I guess I kept doing that. Been doing it for a while.

HOWELL: Is this work you were supposed to have done in college?

BYRNE: And never got around to? (Laughs.) I don't know. It might be a way of working through—not being an end in itself—but of working through how to look at particular things.

HOWELL: In some cases it appears to be pure looking.

BYRNE: Yeah, nothing more than that. Sometimes you just do it, and then print them up, look at them later and see what it is you've been looking at. Or see what exactly Garry Winogrand said—what things look like when you photograph them.

HOWELL: In *True Stories* you had to create things to look at.

BYRNE: Yes, a lot of times it would be partly created and partly mixed with documentary stuff. Or sometimes the created stuff would be an imitation of documentary stuff. The art director would sit with photos of living rooms, and I'd say, "Let's re-create this one and make it look exactly like it does in the photo." And other times we'd try to make everything up.

HOWELL: That was different, I guess, from *Ilé Aiyé*, like the part where those statues twirl. You didn't make up the statues, but you sort of made the scene and made them rotate.

BYRNE: Yeah. In that, it was the editing—putting the two images side by side and playing two things at once—that made it more subjective. You perceived it through the filter of all the editing rather than getting the sense that it was just somebody wandering around with the camera.

HOWELL: One of the things that struck me about *Ilé Aiyé* is that there's so little overt interference—you're not in it. Some people would have loved you to give a five-minute introduction and expose all sorts of personal excitement.

BYRNE: Then it would have become my field trip, my summer vacation.

HOWELL: Was that ever an option?

BYRNE: No, I never considered it, but I did get asked a lot. I can see the reasoning; people thought, "Oh, that's a way to help people get into it." And it would be a selling tool as well.

HOWELL: One of the things that struck me about *Ilé Aiyé* was that there was much more footage of the actual subjects doing what they do. The film does not follow the usual pattern of documentaries, where an authority figure gives a brief history lesson and then provides a voice-over like, "Notice their feet."

BYRNE: The approach is both more and less modern and sophisticated. I thought this way would give you a chance to be more immersed in the music and the lives of the people. And you might have a chance to apprehend the music in the way they would, without all this verbiage and explanation acting as a buffer. You might pick up a little bit of the feeling that they get from it. I think that's easy for what the newspapers call "the MTV generation," the generation that's more visually oriented. In an odd way, we have more in common with these people whose religions and cultures are more sensorial and of the moment. Their religion doesn't have a big text like the Koran or the Bible or anything like that. It's about activity and being physically involved in the present. I think our high-technology has brought us to apprehend things in a similar way.

HOWELL: Was a lot of footage in the documentary found, or were you told about certain events and allowed to film them?

BYRNE: I felt it was important to use a lot of other footage that showed that we weren't shooting one isolated event in place or time and that this stuff has been going on for a long time. The old black-and-white footage gives you that idea that this has been going on for a while—and that it happens in varying ways in different places. The footage has different textures.

> *Some of the film techniques that fell into disuse for fiction films are actually really good for documentaries.*

HOWELL: In order to dive so deeply into another culture—and a very complicated theology—you had to have some structure to begin with, I suppose?

BYRNE: Well, I'd read as much as I could about the religion. I'd gone to things here in New York. And a couple of the compounds in Brazil are sort of open to the public, so you can just go and watch.

HOWELL: Is it common for people to just show up to watch these things?

BYRNE: In some of the places, yeah. Some of the places are bigger and more established and have a parking lot. Groups will show up—a small group of tourists in a VW bus—and will quietly go in and watch.

HOWELL: Do they take donations?

BYRNE: No, they don't take any donations. Not like a church. If you're a member and you're involved and you want something done for you, like a sacrifice or a ritual, then they extract money.

HOWELL: Did you do that?

BYRNE: Yeah, but part of what we were paying for was the right to film, to take people's images and use them for our own ends, and to have sacrifices and rituals performed on our behalf.

HOWELL: Did they know of you? Did they know Talking Heads and your music?

BYRNE: Not very much. In Rio and São Paulo yeah. Not so much in Bahia. Although we did hear "Nothing But Flowers" on the radio once.

HOWELL: How did you hit on the idea of using a little inset screen within the larger frame of the documentary? I can't recall seeing that anywhere.

BYRNE: I've occasionally seen things like that in rock videos. It just seemed like a lot of the film techniques that were used in the sixties—really corny stuff like split-screen graphics and stuff spinning around—work great in documentaries. Instead of having to say, "This is like that," you can put two images side by side and anybody can see the similarity. You can put one thing in a box and the other around it to make an allusion. One thing can refer to the other or one can be a visual subtitle of the other, and you don't have to talk about it. Either you pick up on it or you don't. Some of the film techniques that fell into disuse for fiction films are actually really good for documentaries. It would be best if you could put the little box right in the middle of the frame. In the opening of *Ilé Aiyé* we put the subtitles right in the middle because then it's the easiest to read. You're not looking down and up, down and up, down and up. You can see the subtitles and kind of look through them to the image. But it wasn't possible to do that all the time because some of the subtitles would have been right over people's faces.

HOWELL: Many of your projects have involved collaborations with other artists. Can you talk about collaborating? How do things get done by committee?

BYRNE: It's like the constant improv and refinement in choreography. It can be expanded to include a group. I noticed Twyla Tharp, Bob Wilson, JoAnne Akalaitis and others I've worked with using a similar working method, although sometimes it is interiorized. Working with other humans is great, whether it's Ye Olde Talking Heads or musicians I have worked with recently, like Richard Thompson or Leon Giéco. When you're working on a song with other people, you get to see this more or less one-dimensional thing you come in with expand out in all

When you're working on a song with other people, you get to see this one-dimensional thing expand like a slime mold.

directions like a slime mold. Sometimes you get penicillin; sometimes you get moldy bread, and you have to throw it on the compost heap. I suppose you have to have a deciding voice, a veto vote, in any collaboration. The pretense of democracy is there, but ultimately someone is always deferred to. A unified vision takes precedence over egos, and sometimes the deciding factor changes. On a film score it's obviously the director. I played Bertolucci my impro-

Byrne dances a solo in the Rei Momo video.

visations, and he responded. [*This refers to the score for* The Last
Emperor—*JH*] The final decision was always his. It helps when collaborators use their own judgment, when they trust their own
instincts and don't need to run a test on two thousand teenagers
before they have an opinion. Technically, the collaboration never
ends. The pressing plant and, more importantly, the mastering engineer, also affect the sound of a recording. The field marketing person has an effect on how the work is received, subtly altering the listening experience. The film lab affects the look of a film. The sound
mixer during a performance is a collaborator too.... Phil Glass makes
this obvious by putting Kurt [*Munkasci, Glass's sound engineer—JH*]
on-stage with the rest of the musicians.

HOWELL: Do you prefer working alone or with a group?

BYRNE: There's a time and a place for everything. A piece of shit in the
right place is fertilizer, but in your pants it's an embarrassment...

HOWELL: Listening to *The Catherine Wheel* score, I remembered that
the main reason choreographers don't usually like to use rock-based
music is that it has such a steady rhythm that it limits their choices.
Either you go with it or you work against it; when you work in
between, it gets blurry. Did that come up when you were collaborating with Twyla Tharp on that piece? In some sections the dancers
did work with it.

BYRNE: Yes. In some sections, I'd give them a rhythm and they'd work
with that, and if it was usable, I'd take that rhythm and finish writing the music on top of it. Other times they would have already created, say, three minutes worth of dancing and I'd watch a rehearsal,
or videotape it, then try to write music that would give the impression of being created at the same time or of the music generating the
movement. I tried different rhythms that would make your body
want to move the way the dancers were moving. That was used in a
lot of the African-based stuff in that there were so many rhythms
going on that, no matter which way the dancers moved, they seemed
to be connected with the music. It wasn't a simple four/four boom-
thud, boom-thud.

HOWELL: There were pulses, but there were polyrhythms.

BYRNE: Yeah, they could be dancing to one of the other polyrhythms,
and it would still seem like they were connected to the basic pulse,
even if they weren't. Twyla would say that she definitely did not
always want people dancing on the beat; it made everything look too

square, as if it were blocked off in little eight-bar sections. You start to perceive it that way and your mind starts to close down because it becomes too predictable.

HOWELL: You said earlier that there were several different kinds of stories going on: eight to ten dancers, plus narrative. I can see that the battle would have been to avoid reducing it all to music illustrating movement or movement riding along with music. Have you watched *The Catherine Wheel* recently?

BYRNE: No I haven't, but I listened to the CD a little while ago. I re-edited and re-cued it for the CD, and I was really happy with that. When it was done, I talked with John Rockwell [of the *New York Times*] about the music and he pointed out that, musically, it really did seem to be in little chunks. It was. Some of it would segue into the other, and the dancing was created in little chunks as well. It really is neither a plus nor a minus. It's kind of episodic.

HOWELL: Was he saying that as a criticism?

BYRNE: Yes, he was saying it was a criticism. I think his comment was that somebody like Glenn Branca had a more of a handle on how to create a piece that seemed continuous for fifteen minutes or a half-hour or an hour or whatever—which is true. His would be broken up into much bigger chunks. There'd be five minutes of one kind of drone, then they'd switch to a droning and clanging, then build up to something else. It wasn't totally seamless. I thought that was an interesting comment. Having a long piece like that, you end up working in bigger chunks, like in *The Forest*. One piece will be thirteen minutes long and another will be seven.

HOWELL: Philip Glass's music for dance is in fifteen- or twenty-minute chunks.

BYRNE: And then it shifts gears and switches into something else. A new melody starts, and a new rhythm.

HOWELL: But Twyla's dance had more variety in it, too. She had several things going on there, including a narrative, which most dances don't attempt.

BYRNE: That's right. For a few years there, she was experimenting and incorporating narrative things.

HOWELL: Was it difficult, scoring something for the first time?

BYRNE: Well, maybe half of that music was done to order. Like I said, I'd either watch a rehearsal or a video and write something to fit. That was the first time I learned to discipline myself to do that.

HOWELL: And be for hire.

BYRNE: Which was fun. I really liked it. It's sometimes nice to be reined in.

HOWELL: You haven't really worked with dance *per se* on that scale since you worked with Twyla. Has that been a consequence of circumstance, or did people ask and you not find the occasion?

BYRNE: That was a big project. It was a fairly long piece and she knew she wanted to do a whole theater-type production on Broadway. There haven't been too many of those kinds of things attempted since then.

HOWELL: So people think you're out for really big deals.

BYRNE: Only big deals. Doing the film stuff is similar in the fact that it's music-for-hire for a specific thing. When I started putting the stage show together for the *Stop Making Sense* tour, I was applying some of the stuff I had absorbed from working with Twyla, like how to organize a stage presentation.

HOWELL: When you were presented with *The Last Emperor* as a movie to score, did you immerse yourself in Chinese music?

BYRNE: Yeah. I got whatever records I could get in the United States and Bernardo and the film people gave me stacks of cassettes that they had gotten in China and Hong Kong. I listened to them and made notes, and filtered it down. The big surprise to me was that there is such a wide range in Chinese music. It's a huge country! There's music we're more familiar with—Western-sounding, women-staged operas. Then there's really austere folk and classical music, where just one stringed instrument plucks a note occasionally, like Japanese classical music.

Bernardo and the film people gave me stacks of cassettes that they had gotten in China and Hong Kong.

But the Chinese would write piano pieces in which they'd amalgamate Twentieth Century music with traditional Chinese music. It sounds like Stravinsky-goes-Chinese.

HOWELL: What was your cue for developing musical themes for *The Last Emperor*? Did you read the story?

BYRNE: I just read the script. I saw the first cut of the movie, which was five hours long, and then I'd see progressive cuts after that. That's really what I was working with—not the story, but the way they interpreted it.

HOWELL: Did Bertolucci parcel out scenes to you and your co-composers, Cong Su and Ryuichi Sakamoto?

BYRNE: Yes. Because of the film's time schedule, they needed everything as soon as possible. Sakamoto and I were both in the middle of making records so that we each had only a few weeks here and there to devote to it. Both of us kept sending Bernardo demos. Every week or two I sent things that sounded more or less Chinese—some would sound more Chinese and some would sound less because I didn't know how far he wanted to go with it. We had agreed that the music had to help make you feel like you were seeing something in China, although we knew we didn't want *chinoiserie*.

HOWELL: Fake China?

BYRNE: Yeah, he didn't want "Dink-dink-dink-dink-dink" [*sings in a hokey Chinese style*] like those old Hollywood movie scores. He would assign scenes. The working process was that I would look at them on video and play on the emulator, imitating Chinese instruments of different kinds. I tried different kinds of things very crudely because I'm not a keyboard player, but I'd just plunk out a crude melody or texture. Bernardo would listen to it and say yea or nay. Most of the time he liked what I did. There were a couple scenes I didn't believe, so I could never come up with anything that satisfied any of us. Or my take on what I was seeing and the resulting musical interpretation was completely different from the way Bernardo wanted the scene to come across.

HOWELL: Do you think that *The Last Emperor* is a conventional narrative?

BYRNE: Parts of it. In the sense that it follows one guy all the way through, it is. Also in the Hollywood sense of the main character having an obvious conflict that gets resolved. But it's not as simple as that. It's made up of all these disjointed things happening one after another.

HOWELL: Let's talk about the theater piece by Robert Wilson that you scored, *The Forest*. You were attempting to develop a film version of it.

BYRNE: The film went into limbo. Eventually it was decided that the theater production would be Bob's and that I would do a film interpretation of the story. But it wouldn't be an interpretation of the stage piece; it would be completely different, taking the same story and going off on another tangent. I worked up a scene-by-scene scenario to the point where I'd say, "This scene is going to take place in this kind of location and then this happens." I didn't have any dialogue or text, but I knew what was going to happen. Unfortunately, I was muddled up about the end. I didn't quite know

Following the taping of a scene for the Rei Momo video, Byrne reviews the shot.

how to tie things together. But I had enough funding to drive around Germany and scout locations. But because Germany was so heavily bombed during the wars, there's not a lot of stuff left from the 1850s. So to get one exterior we'd have to go to the South of Germany, and for another we'd have to go to the North. Traveling around the country to make everything look authentic was too expensive. It was a daunting problem. The budget—seven million U.S. dollars—was high for an art movie.

HOWELL: Did they know the epic of Gilgamesh in Germany?

BYRNE: Some people did. Not a whole lot of people, but some. And it seemed a nice gesture to set it in Germany since they were going to put up a fair amount of the money. Now I can't imagine that it could ever be done in England or in America. I always imagined that it should have a feeling that seems kind of foreign to us. I worked with a screenwriter named Michael Hearst, who has written stuff for Nick Roeg and John Boorman and some other British directors. He more or less finished a script, but we never got to the end. We kept having meetings and revising it, but we never got the ending resolved. It's still just sitting there. I think it's a neat story; and the way we dealt with it was very interesting, but because of the money I don't think it will ever be done in that form.

HOWELL: The way you focused *The Forest* to contrast civilization and nature, the more uniquely German it seemed to become. That has been a deep contradiction in German culture, and it is also a current debate because their forests are disappearing.

BYRNE: The more I did research on Germany during the Industrial Revolution, the more it seemed that the whole concern is currently replaying itself, with the industrialists taking one side and the romantics taking the other. It was an education for me. A lot of what we tend to consider modern, Twentieth Century thought came about during that period. Like the idea of traveling to see nature, to look at the mountains or the ocean or big vistas. We do that. We go on vacations to Italy to see romantic villages. That romanticization of nature and of a simple life seems to have come out of a reaction to the Industrial Revolution. You can trace it even further back if you want to. We still work from those assumptions, even though we might try to throw them off. I can be kind of cynical about it, but I'm as susceptible to it as anyone. I do the same thing; I go to the mountains and see the big vistas, and I'm awestruck.

HOWELL: You mentioned that you listened to a lot of the music from that period. Mahler?

BYRNE: Yes. I tried to steep myself in it. Mahler's a little bit later, but I thought, "Oh, this is pretty Romantic-sounding to me." I listened to Brahms, Bruckner, Sibelius. Those are a little bit later, too. And I also listened to Wagner. I just don't get a lot of Wagner.

HOWELL: I was just listening to one of his pieces that starts with a low horn and swells up and then...

BYRNE: Those bits of it I get. It sounds like it's going to be a sound track for *The Ten Commandments* or something like that.

HOWELL: Something huge. What was the German reaction to what you were doing?

BYRNE: The younger people seemed kind of surprised that I was interested in any of this. A large part of the young community is in Kreuzberg; it's kind of the Lower East Side of Berlin. Almost everybody in that part of town dresses in black and wears sunglasses at night. They like things that are grungy and real and cynical. They tend to go for music like Nick Cave and Bad Seeds and Einsturzende Neubaten, who were in the studio when I was there. They wandered in and out, bringing pieces of plumbing...

HOWELL: ... chain saws...

BYRNE: It looked like they got all their instruments on Canal Street. They'd carry big industrial sinks into the elevator and into the studio. It really sounded great. They had all this stuff just hanging around inside the studio and they'd bang on it.

HOWELL: In the meantime, you were quietly listening to Mahler on your headphones.

BYRNE: To me, it's almost the same thing. What they're doing is romantic in its own way. It's romanticizing angst. Nihilism romanticizes the failure. It puts it in quotes. So I thought it was really similar to Mahler, even though on the surface it couldn't be more different, which is what I was saying to

I am convinced that all this corny Romanticism is the foundation of a lot of art and music.

them. I wasn't trying to convince them, "Hey, I'm hip, I'm doing the same thing that you're doing, but it just happens to be with an orchestra." I am convinced that all this corny Romanticism is the foundation of a lot of art and music. It's just retold in new languages.

Byrne reviewing the tape with his director of photography.

HOWELL: Was scoring music for an orchestra difficult? It's not exactly your specialty, is it?

BYRNE: I wasn't trained in music; I didn't go to music school and learn the ins and outs of musical composition. So when I was making this music, it was a naive take on it.

HOWELL: How did you tell the musicians what to do? They were symphonic musicians?

BYRNE: I had a go-between again, a Los Angeles arranger named Jimmy Haskell. He mainly does sound tracks and pop songs; but he's used to working with people like myself who don't know the technical language of music but can describe what we want. He translates that into musical language and either communicates with the musicians or writes it on the score. I could just say, "I want more feeling in this," or, "this is too loud," or, "this is too quiet," or, "let's drop the violins down an octave because they sound too separate from the brass instruments." In a way, I thought my naivete might work to my advantage. I'll never know for sure if it did or didn't because I was redoing it on my own terms, rewriting Wagner or Mahler, taking out all the stuff that I didn't really get and keeping all the stuff I liked. If I had understood their music perfectly, I wouldn't have dared to attempt rewriting it.

HOWELL: Your use of this mix of musical forms from around the world brings us back to something we talked about earlier: deliberate but inevitable misunderstandings of Third World culture, due to a naive Western take on it.

BYRNE: Yes. You could say the same thing about listening to African music and hearing it on your own terms. Obviously I try to educate myself about it as much as I can, but I'm never going to see it and hear it the same way that Africans did or do. It's always going to be filtered through some prism and come out different on the other side, but I assume that's how they did it too. They were hearing something else and trying to get a musical effect or a create a musical feeling, and what they ended up with was a misunderstanding or a reinterpretation of something on their own terms.

HOWELL: When you worked on *The Last Emperor*, you immersed yourself in Chinese music, and when you worked on *The Forest*, you borrowed from Mahler and Wagner and German Romanticism. But when you did Robert Wilson's *The Knee Plays*, you started with Japanese music, then ditched it and went to New Orleans.

BYRNE: Yeah, well, the whole show had a more of a Japanese flavor to it than it might have because the workshops were done in Japan. There's an obvious similarity between a lot of traditional Japanese theater and modern theater from the last twenty years or so. Bob Wilson's slow-motion stuff is similar to a lot of Noh: people posing, moving really slowly, and then a gesture. The whole approach to drama is very similar except that the Japanese base theirs on stories, while Bob's are often purely images and text and sound. The Japanese plays have a story, but half the time the audience can't understand what the people are saying in Kabuki or Noh. Sometimes they follow along in their programs, but often they're just looking for beautiful posing, costumes, and the stage pictures. So I wanted to mix those similarities together. I started off with the requirements of the piece. There would be five-minute interludes between the big acts; they would have to come on-stage really quickly, perform, and go off again when the sets were changed for the next act. The music had to cover up the noises of hammering or sawing or pushing big wooden props behind the curtain. It had to be percussive. First I thought, "Oh, I'll work with Japanese percussionists," and it ended up sounding like the Japanese equivalent of *chinoiserie*. Sometimes I did some stuff on my own, but it was terrible. It sounded Japan-esque. So I decided to go to the opposite extreme. I remembered that when I'd seen the Dirty Dozen [a New Orleans brass band], there were elements that were funky and earthy, and it still had a hypnotic quality. They take a riff and repeat it and repeat it and repeat it. I thought that might work in juxtaposition to the texture and pace of Bob's stage stuff. I thought it would be great as an experiment, anyway, to try to put some funkiness against that ethereal drama which often was reduced to just a gesture or an eyebrow arch. I already knew that Phil Glass's music worked perfectly with Bob's stuff, so I thought, "Let's try something else. Let's see if putting a different kind of music against it creates a different mood."

HOWELL: Obviously it must have worked. *The Knee Plays* have been touring for two or three years. Part of that may be because it is one of Bob's economical pieces.

BYRNE: Yes, that was the idea. One of the main reasons I got involved with *The Knee Plays* was because I realized, "This one can tour and actually be seen; it can be a little package that can move around."

Byrne on vocals and rhythm guitar, with the backbeat by Tina Weymouth on bass and lead guitar by Adrian Belew.

A lot of the bigger sections of *the CIVIL warS* got so involved and expensive that the whole piece was never finished.

HOWELL: Do you feel that these types of projects have alienated you from your rock audience?

BYRNE: That I've just gone off and lost them? That I'm doing something over here, and the audience feels, "He's off on his own now?"

HOWELL: Yeah. Has your celebrity persona created a barrier between you and the audience? People have such strong expectations of you based on your track record; and then when you do something different, audiences act surprised.

BYRNE: Or offended.

HOWELL: Or puzzled. I remember the reaction to Talking Heads's *Little Creatures*. Some people complained: "You were innovative for so long, and now you're doing gospel music and Cajun stuff." Some people found it delightful, and other people said, "Anybody could have done that; those forms have been here forever."

BYRNE: That's true. They're both true.

HOWELL: Do you think the popular perception of David Byrne as a star creates a barrier or distances you from your audience?

BYRNE: Maybe there's a barrier in the public's mind. Nothing is shielding me, though. The public likes their myths to live in a never-never land, not in the real world. I'm aware that celebs serve as a collective dream of the public and that *People* magazine is the national Dream Book. We aim to please. God help us if we disappoint, as I must have done numerous times in the last few years.... I have to follow my own instincts, and they're not that different from what other people may be feeling. If I am infatuated with Latin music, it shouldn't be surprising. It's not that different from a lot of the African stuff that Talking Heads did. I did a similar thing for *Something Wild;* it's not a radical jump, it's just more of it. You were saying that pop music is amorphous; it stretches pretty far. You can stretch it enough to include some of this Latin stuff or African stuff. Just think of it as popular music.

> *The public likes their myths to live in a never-never land, not in the real world.*

HOWELL: What about when you move over into Mahler and Wagner?

BYRNE: I don't know what that is anymore.

HOWELL: I was listening to music from *The Forest*, and I wonder if anyone would know that you did it.

BYRNE: I don't think they would know, really.

HOWELL: Do you ever have the desire to drop out of sight and become totally anonymous?

BYRNE: Well, I was just in Madras, South India. Didn't exactly sign a lot of autographs there. The public likes us with face lifts, skinny noses and perfect bods. Troubled and tortured in our magic castles. Get real.

HOWELL: Do you have any advice for aspiring musicians who are making music outside the mainstream?

BYRNE: Don't listen to people who give advice. That's my advice.

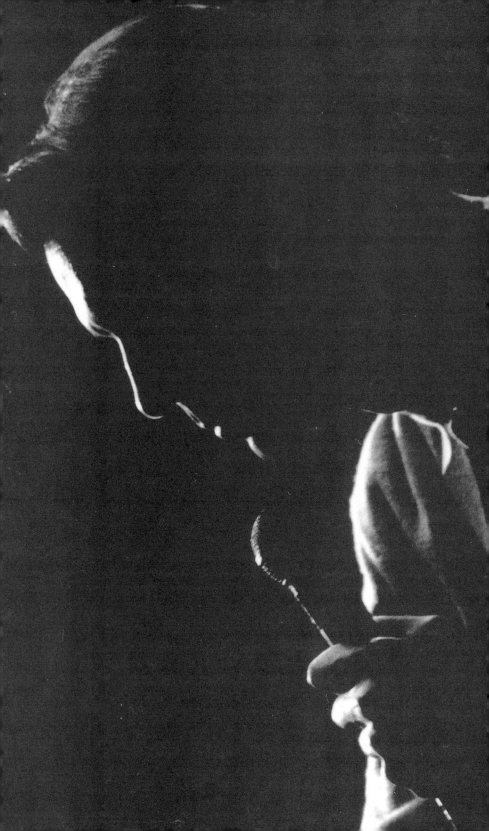

NEW RELEASE

PHOTOGRAPHS BY DAVID BYRNE

Byrne (page left) performing a cover version of Led Zeppelin's "Whole Lotta Love" (karaoke style), at a fundraiser at the Tunnel, New York City.

Untitled
6 1/2 x 9 7/8"
color coupler print

Vending Machines on the Street Corner, Tokyo
6 1/2 x 9 7/8"
color coupler print

Real Estate Office, Roppongi, Tokyo
6 1/2 X 9 7/8"
color coupler print

Untitled
6 1/2 x 9 7/8"
color coupler print

Neighborhood Map and Coke Machine, Tokyo
6 1/2 x 9 7/8"
color coupler print

Untitled
6 1/2 x 9 7/8"
color coupler print

Warning Sign, Construction Site, Tokyo
6 1/2 x 9 7/8"
color coupler print

Building Lobby, Tokyo
6 1/2 x 9 7/8"
color coupler print

Set for New Year T.V. Special, Hong Kong
9 7/8 x 6 1/2"
color coupler print

Set for New Year T.V. Special, Hong Kong
9 7/8 x 6 1/2"
color coupler print

David Byrne, the man in media, becomes the man in motion on a lead guitar riff.

THE *REI MOMO*
TOUR DIARY

A fter recording *Rei Momo* in 1989, an album influenced by Latin rhythms and arrangements, Byrne set out to present the music on stage. The tour was to include a swing through South America as well as the United States, a choice Byrne felt was vital if his ambition to demonstrate a true cross-cultural spirit was to succeed. Despite doubts on the part of his record company, and the logistical difficulties, Byrne hit the road in the late spring. Aware that he was launching himself into an adventure in cultural understanding as well as presenting a concert, he kept a taped diary of his travels. What follows is an abridged version of that diary.

THE *REI MOMO*
TOUR DIARY

BY DAVID BYRNE

made a record [*Rei Momo*] during the spring and summer of 1989
with a number of Latin and Brazilian musicians. I felt that the
resulting record, although it had strong songs, was an unusual
mixture. It was probably too Anglo for the Latin radio stations and
definitely too Latin for the rock stations that used to play Talking
Heads. For that reason I assumed that it would be a good idea to put
this new sound in front of the public as soon as possible.

So, I put together a sixteen-piece band that could play all the Latin
and Brazilian styles and some of the rockier Talking Heads stuff as
well. In late September we began our tour-proper in Japan, moving
east across the United States and ending in Europe by Christmas.

I had a great time playing this music, and I really wanted to take
the show to Central and South America, where audiences might be
more familiar with the rhythms. I wanted them to hear first-hand
what we were doing, and if there were to be any criticisms or com-
plaints, I would be there to take them, face to face.

It proved to be difficult to put this tour together. I'm not a big star
in Latin America. Talking Heads never had any hot singles, although
both they and I were not totally unknown. Amelia Lafferriere, a woman
who had sent me lots of recordings of Argentine folkloric stuff, introduced me to some producers who had previously put together a tour
for Mercedes Sosa, an artist who has high principals and standards.

These guys were the only agents I talked to who felt this thing could be done. So we were on our way.

SAN JUAN, PUERTO RICO

Old San Juan reminded me a bit of Salvador, Bahia, in that there was an old colonial town surrounded by modern condos, hotels and shantytowns as well. I stopped at a roadside food stall where people were eating on their lunch break, and I asked someone what one of the dishes was. It was stomach salad—bits of stomach, olives, onions. So I tried some of that with rice and beans, *platanos* and a Perrier water.

As I walked around town I stumbled upon two record stores in Old San Juan, one of which was a combination record and book store. I expected maybe, oh, the current American rock-and-roll Top Forty, and the equivalent in Latin music, salsa, some merengues, and the current popular Latin-romantic-erotic ballads from people like Roberto Carlos. But the selection at these shops was not limited to that at all. The choices seemed to have been made by the owners of the shops. My Brazilian compilations were on display. There were a lot of Cuban things. A lot of *nuevo cancion*. Of course, they did have the American Top Forty. They had a lot of jazz. A lot of Brazilian material. Both stores had lots of records—Milton Nascimento and Caetano Velosa and everybody like that. I guess you could say it was an interesting cross-section of the music of the Americas. Very culturally aware. Very politically aware.

I picked up a CD by Victor Jara from Chile, whose work I was unfamiliar with. And the sales clerk was telling me how, when Pinochet came to power, they cut off Victor Jara's hands.

The first show in San Juan went okay. It was the first show with our new percussionists—some numbers went a little too fast, some numbers a little too slow. Not everything was played with total confidence in the rhythm department.

What was strange was that almost the entire audience were guests of the Ponce de Leon Bank, which had paid the promoter for a very large percentage of that night's tickets. They had given them out as presents to the secretaries and various people in the offices, some of whom came, were very interested and had a great time. Others who came were not interested at all. There were lots and lots of empty seats—I guess from people who just weren't even interested enough to show up. So it was a strange experience.

I took solace in the fact that Celia Cruz, who was also in town, was playing to a secretaries convention the day before we got in. So, apparently, those kinds of performances are not rare here.

Last night's performance, the second one in San Juan, was completely different. It was like another world, like we were playing for a completely different audience. They were incredibly receptive, from the very first number by Margareth [Menezes, the Brazilian popular singer who toured with the *Rei Momo* band]. When I announced, in Spanish, that we were doing a bomba—knowing that it was a rhythm of Puerto Rico—there was a huge cheer. And to top it all off, Celia Cruz, introduced simply as *"La Reina"* ("the Queen"), showed up and came on stage to sing "Loco de Amor" with me. The minute she hit the stage the whole audience was on its feet. Before she sang a note, there was a three-minute standing ovation from an audience that was probably as much into rock-and-roll as they were into Latin music. It was an incredible thrill.

After our last song, "Make Believe Mambo," we left the stage, and the audience was all singing, "Todo mundo, mundo mambo/Todo mundo, mundo mambo...." They kept it going until we got back; and then we had to start the next song, which was in a completely different tempo, with this chant ringing in our ears. A kind of wonderful challenge.

TUESDAY

Wow! What a night. The promoter drastically over-sold the theater, and there was a line around the block that just wouldn't quit. Ladysmith Black Mambazo was the opening act. It was very, very nice. The place was packed, and they were still letting people in. So it was turning into a sweatbox. Margareth goes through her first number, and all of a sudden I get worried because the fire marshall has said that the show can't go on unless one hundred people leave. Well, that's very sweet. How do we resolve this?

So I go onstage and make the announcement. The audience is very upset! First we get the stage manager on, who doesn't really help out at all. The promoter's initial response is to offer one hundred people their money back. I tell him he's got to do better, otherwise nobody's going to leave after they've been sitting in this place for hours, sweating, waiting for a show. So we suggest to him that he offer transportation and tickets to the show tomorrow night in Gainesville. There are a few takers for this—people who are probably just disgusted by being squashed into this hot-box and want to see the show under maybe, possibly more pleasant circumstances. But it becomes clear that he's got to offer better. He feels like he doesn't want to do anything.

We push him on a little bit further, and he offers double the money back and transportation to Gainesville. This gets takers, and after waiting maybe fifteen minutes, the show goes back on, to a very, very good response. It was in this morning's paper, the problems, but no mention about how good the show was....

GAINESVILLE, FLORIDA: NEXT DAY

Okay, the show in Gainesville. It went great. The crew was very tired but much happier that all the equipment worked, that they had a big enough monitor board, a big enough mixing board, more or less enough lights. Everything sort of worked. And so they were happier than they had been for a while. And the show went over really well. The audience was excited.

MEXICO CITY: TUESDAY, APRIL 29

The promoter takes us out to eat at a very nice restaurant. Walking distance from the hotel...Wonderful Mexican food. Tortillas with a fungus spread inside. Little baked corn things with beans and things on top. Bottles of tequila on the table with some *gritta*, a kind of alcohol-free Bloody Mary mix to cut it with.

And as far as this stuff goes, so far, Mexico is the shining star! They've been very, very nice to us here.

MEXICO CITY: WEDNESDAY, APRIL 30

The next day I spent a good part of the day doing interviews in a little conference room in the hotel. The interviewers were very nice.

A song playlist, with notes, during the soundcheck on the Rei Momo tour.

They were a mixture of people from the Tropical radio station, Tropicoo, and a lot of people from rock radio stations and other reporters, and they were coming in one or two at a time.

Then, in the afternoon, we went out to one of the top rock radio stations—one of the sponsors of the concert, I believe—doing a lot of promotion. And although they only have one tropical hour radio program, they have been playing my record. There were occasionally presented problems when I'd make requests for a merengue group or something else. They wouldn't have the records! But they did have Elvis Costello and other kinds of things.

They spoke of what they called the Trans Culture, a culture of the young people in Mexico who speak a lot of English, listen to American music. We talked about it going back the other way.

I had asked if they knew about a record store that sold Tropical Music. I was taken to one in the suburbs in the south. It was getting on to rush hour, the traffic was getting pretty bad. It was a small store that sold exclusively, for want of a better word, salsa records. And it had probably every record Willie Colon had ever made. And obscure records from the sixties by Larry Harlow. A whole rack of Cuban records. Los Van Van and obscure Cuban collections that I'd never heard of. I bought some CD collections of old stuff. Perez Prado on RCA. They are some of the better recordings.

The man who owned the store and was behind the counter was dressed in a gray polyester suit with red stitching. He looked quite nice. It was a slightly flashy look but very tailored as well. He thanked us profusely, wished me well in the concert, thanked me for helping promote The Music, and we were on our way.

I rested back here at the hotel for about an hour or so. And we all went to a club, disco, whatever you want to call it, where the whole band did a press conference. I introduced the band in Spanish as best I could. Everyone sat on sort of a stage, groups of two or three of us around small tables on the stage, each with a microphone and a glass of water and Coca-Cola on the table.

They started asking questions. With most of the attention on me, I would respond in English, the moderator would translate. Eventually, I asked that they address some questions to the band. I felt it was incredibly insulting to them, and besides, here were all these great musicians who knew a lot more about the music than me, and who could articulate from that point of view what it was like for us all to work together.

The questions were sometimes way out from left field. One man, I assume referring to "City of Dreams" from the Talking Heads record, *True Stories*, said that although I seemed sympathetic to the plight of Native Americans, wasn't I in fact making money off their plight by writing a song about it? It's kind of like the question, "When did you stop beating your wife?" You are presumed guilty by the fact that you are asked the question.

There were a few questions like that, and there were a few other kind of unexpected moments. There were beautiful moments when the band defended me from insinuations that I was watering down The Music and defended what we were doing, defended the idea of Latin, Tropical or Brazilian music being sung in English. I was very flattered. Basically we were putting forth the idea that we shouldn't feel boxed in. We shouldn't feel that the music or the rhythms are limited to, and can only be played by, one people.

The thing went on longer than we'd hoped. I got mobbed by autograph-seekers afterwards, was handed a bunch of cassettes (some of which looked really interesting!) and made an escape.

MEXICO CITY: THURSDAY, MAY 3

Tonight is our first show here. It's sold out. I believe that the venue is a large bandshell with an outdoor audience, like the Hollywood Bowl, that holds about six thousand. I'm impressed! I've heard the radio ads, which are really good. They're running on at least two stations and make no effort to disguise the fact that we're playing Tropical Music as radio ads in other parts of the world have done.

Later, same day.

I've been doing Brazilian phone interviews for the last hour. They inevitably ask some of the same questions. It gets to sound like a broken record.

Took a walk in downtown Mexico City, where I'd been a few years earlier. It reminds me a little bit of downtown Rio. Walked down the street from the hotel, caught the subway, which is very clean, quiet, no graffiti, no dirt. If only New Yorkers and Americans knew that countries like Mexico can run things better than New York can, they'd be amazed. They might lose a little bit of their haughtiness.

I saw a man with very Aztec features, with a shaved head, a

Brass added depth and power to the Rei Momo sound.

Mexican Hare Krishna, judging by his robes. He was standing outside a stall where a girl was selling candies and stuffed animals in the Metro station. Brilliant pastel colors. And this guy was chatting up the sales girl. It was one of the strangest images I had ever seen. The old part of the city is incredible. The streets are filled with people. The shop windows are filled with all sorts of merchandise. There's a real liveliness and hustle and bustle.

Later, evening.

I've just returned from the show here in Mexico City, and although their presentation, the hotel and restaurants and everything else they took us to was very nice, the show was totally chaotic. The PA was inadequate. They couldn't get the lights together. It took them all night, twenty-four hours. Pete Jennings, our lighting guy, stayed until seven in the morning, when of course, it was light, and he couldn't do anything because he couldn't see the effect that the lights were having due to the sun. And they still had not gotten it right. So he went back to the hotel.

Just before we went on, maybe half-an-hour before the audience was starting to pour in, there was a torrential downpour, a thunderstorm that didn't let up for about an hour. Well, the people didn't leave! They just screamed and hollered. And the equipment was getting soaked, things were shorting out, fuses were blowing, the PA went down, the lights went down, the lights came back on, the PA came back on, announcements were made.... People would stumble back into the dressing room totally drenched, then they'd stumble back out again.

The equipment was not grounded, and so if it got totally soaked again in a downpour, there was a good chance that the high voltage for the PA could travel through the microphones and electrocute us all. So we had to wait until the rain started to let up. And the audience waited. It must have been just about six thousand totally soaked people, at least the ones that weren't under the canopy.

We were in a kind of parabolic bandshell that was the worst possible thing for sound, for the kind of music we were doing. For example, Lewis Kahn could play his violin at one end of the stage; an amplified version of it was heard by Ray Martinez, who was playing bass at the opposite end of the stage, and no one else could hear it.

It would bounce up to this overhanging lip and reflect down, focused to a pinpoint, at some obscure location on some hapless musician on the other end of the stage. Everyone in the band was hearing a different, bizarrely balanced mix of instruments. There was no way to correct all this. We could barely keep it together with the rhythm because it was like playing in an aural swamp.

The audience seemed to love it. Of course, they reacted strongly to songs they knew. Margareth got a very good reception. When we played "Loco de Amor" they knew all the words in the chorus. "Burning Down the House" got a great reception. "Make Believe Mambo" got a great reception.

I think it was successful, but at one point the whole side of the PA sparked and went into flames. We saw a parade of young firemen, all in matching red outfits, galloping across the back of the stage with their fire extinguishers, attempting to put out the right side of the PA. As an emergency measure Vance Anderson [production manager and sound man] attempted to pan all the instruments to the left side! So at this point the crowd must have heard the group only from one side, in one ear. But of course, things being what they were, he wasn't entirely successful. He did the best he could, but no one seemed to mind. We'll see what people say tomorrow in the papers.

The audience continued to be very receptive and I felt obliged to compete with the energy that the audience had put out. And being that we're at an altitude of at least a mile high, I found myself getting winded occasionally. But it was an exciting or pleasurable kind of pain and a challenge to push yourself, push your stamina to its limits. I could barely catch my breath sometimes to just sing the next line in some of the songs, after dancing around all over the stage.

MIAMI, FLORIDA

We played our first show here last night, and it was the first show that's gone really well musically. My wife Bonny and our one-year-old daughter, Malu, are here. They met us at the airport when we arrived from Mexico City. We rented a car and drove into a little Deco hotel that the promoter has us in.

During yesterday afternoon, I had numerous talks on the beach, by the pool, in the hotel with different members of the band, concerned about the rhythm and the tempos. I talked with them, and said, "We're going to do a long sound check and really rehearse and go over everything."

Which we did. We did a soundcheck for about an hour-and-a-half maybe. Very, very productive. It sounded great, with all the tempos locked in, more or less.

During the performance that evening it was incredibly hot on stage. Everyone in the band was drenched with sweat. Everyone could see right through Margareth's dress. Ray was playing bass like a man in a trance, he couldn't take his eyes off her. There were times when I could barely breathe, barely stand up, felt like I was going to faint. But somehow we got through it all. And the audience loved it! They were pretty much drenched with sweat as well.

MIAMI: TUESDAY

We go back to do the second show in Miami, which went... Well, in retrospect, it went over really well, but I was very upset. The tempos were not as steady or as strong as they were Saturday night, and I started getting really upset because the night before, most of the tempos were good. We spent a long soundcheck going over the other numbers that needed a little bit of work. And I thought I'd covered everything, but everything seemed to fall apart in the show. The audience seemed to like it very much. Some said, of course, that it sounded better than the night before!

Charlie Negrita, Cafe [percussionist] and I worked out a version of "Psycho Killer" during sound check which we did as a prelude for the second encore. The instrumentation was berimbau, conga and acoustic guitar, and it sounds like it's going to work. It was kind of sloppy, but all right.

We did suffer another disaster this night. Just as we had formed a circle and done our little cheer before Margareth and company went on to do "Elejibo," the song from Bahia that she performs with percussion as a show opener, a man comes running out of the stage approach area, yelling, "Fire." It turns out that all the air conditioning pumps that had been running all day, keeping the place a little bit cooler than the night before, burst into flame. An electrical fire. A bunch of guys rushing on with fire extinguishers, and this horrible smell of burning rubber and wire, kind of choking everyone in our area. The audience seems unaware of it. The fire is extinguished after a few minutes, and after maybe ten or fifteen minutes we do go on. But of course, the air conditioning once again is not working and we're plunged into another night of incredible heat. The kind of heat where you can barely breathe and barely get through the numbers. It's like a contest of how much you can endure.

I manage to squeeze in a meeting, a chat with an old friend, who is now an A & R man for Warner Brothers. He saw both shows in Miami, loved them, was impressed with the audience reaction, and wonders why our record company hasn't done more to capitalize on the public's reaction to this tour. He enjoyed the show very much. Apparently he had never seen it before. Now that he's seen it get over to the general public, a public not one hundred percent familiar with Latin music, he is convinced that the music is accessible.

I am quite happy, for the moment, to work at a more or less grass roots level, building from a base of audience support and enthusiasm that might eventually translate in years to come into radio play and record sales.

RIO DE JANEIRO, BRAZIL

The beach in front of our hotel has a small black river running into it; the favela (shantytown) perched on the hill has no public sewage, so all of their waste runs right down the hill, through a concrete gully, and into the ocean—right in front of this fancy hotel. I join Margareth and her friend, and we drive south to a spot with a clean beach. It's almost deserted. The sea is rough, so after a short swim, we return.

The show was very good. The audience was as good as they could be in a kind of formal, seated theatre like the Teatro Nacional. They were up and dancing from about the second or third song. Some of the other ones took it as a formal occasion. The applause here in Rio, as it would be in Sao Paulo, would be intense and then drop off dramatically, so that rather than fading down, as it often does after a song, it suddenly dropped off to be almost nothing, as if the audience was saying, "Okay, you've had your applause; now we're ready for another number." And I would sometimes have to talk for a minute in my garbled Portuñol (a combination of Portuguese and Spanish) to try and give the band a second to switch their instruments and turn the pages on their music sheets or whatever, get a drink of water, wipe themselves off with a towel (it was quite hot).

After the Rio show, Steve Sandberg, our synthesizer player, and I had a little talk about how our audience, due to the ticket price, was almost entirely white, that we were obviously playing to a very small segment, a very limited cross section, of the Rio population.

Some friends came backstage. Caetano Veloso's wife, Paulinha, and teen-age son missed his show across town (he's playing a week's run) to check us out. Silly that we're both playing the same night. He's doing one of my songs, "Nothing But Flowers," and I'm doing one popularized by him, "Um Canto Do Ilé Passar, " We talk before the show and agree to meet at a restaurant later after our shows. The conversation concerns a new "novela" or soap opera shot in a beautiful region and featuring a fair amount of nudity.

SAO PAULO, BRAZIL: NEXT DAY

The day of the show, I slept very late, then went out with Lewis Kahn and Steve Sacks to try to find some Brazilian records that might not be available in the States—which we did. We spent almost all our pocket money.

Went to the venue and did a sound check. It's a large converted warehouse with a stage at one end. It seems more appropriate to our show than the place that had been booked in Rio. Anyway, the audience can dance, move about, get something to drink.

The show goes on late; ten o'clock is the actual beginning. A couple of numbers were too fast maybe. Some tempos wavered a little bit. But on the whole, it was quite good. The audience response was good. The band felt excited.

Some fans left some books in my room. One is a picture book of houses in the Northeast called *Pinturas e Platibandas*, by Anna Mariani. These houses are beautiful. As are her photos. It's the style Duncan and I used to call Brazilian Futurism—kind of a naive, geometrical tropical style that we've never seen anywhere else. Beautiful stuff.

© F-STOP FITZGERALD

An assortment of drums and drummers provided "sabor" (flavor) on the Rei Momo tour.

More rhythm and "sabor" with drums.

It's my birthday. I'm in Curitiba. We played two more dates in Sao Paulo. The second date in São Paulo went very well, better than the first. It was videotaped by MTV-Brazil, which is just starting up, and this is a means for them to get some material for the Brazilian market. I went to visit Tom Zé in São Paulo on Saturday afternoon. He tells a wonderful story about what his dreams for his music are. In this story, he talks about the ring of mostly poor immigrants who have settled in the suburbs around São Paulo. People from the Northeast, which is where he comes from as well. He says that São Paulo could be called the largest city in the Northeast. That these people for three hundred years have been undernourished, for nine generations they've been undernourished and not had enough protein for their brains. Now if they make a little money, they receive more protein, and their brains become starved for stimulus. And what do they get? They get television, soap operas.

I visited a kind of crafts bazaar in the square. There were a few Northeasterners, some Bahianas—women from Bahia—all dressed in white, selling *acarajé, caruru* and *vatapá,* the African-derived foods of the Northeast. So I order that for lunch. I miss Bahia, I was so moved by my stay there a couple of years ago. On the way back to the hotel, I stop at another stall and buy a white neckalce in association with my Orisha, Oshala—or Obatala as he is called in Santeria.

That night, Saturday, we came back from our show, and in our hotel there is an advertised, open jam featuring the blues musicians who have been playing in another part of town. Magic Slim, Bo Diddley, the Kinsey Report, John Hammond, some others. The bar and lounge area on the second floor of the hotel is packed with people. There is a drum setup, some amps, a piano, not much else. Joe Crifo, one of our stagehands, plays drums quite well, so the two of us are hanging out waiting for someone to play or for something to happen.

Somebody hands me a guitar. A bass player appears, a drummer appears. We play for about half-an-hour, the same chord but different grooves—maybe two chords. More or less funk-blues, as is my leaning. I certainly can't play lead, so I opt for kind of funky rhythms. We're all wedged into this little alcove in the lounge. Joe somehow manages to relieve the drummer who was playing without missing a beat. He seemed to take over one hand at a time, until eventually he was in command of the whole kit. And that kicks off the night of blues jamming.

PORTO ALEGRE, BRAZIL: TUESDAY, MAY 15

Last night's show in Curitiba was the first with Oscar Salas [a new percussionist and drummer]. Some songs went really well, and on some songs he played more a rock or jazz style than Latin, to our surprise. We went over every rhythm in soundcheck, but it was difficult for him to remember every break and every stop and every change. He did pretty well. There was a good energy.

At any rate, the tempos were steady. And occasionally, I feel here is a pointer as to where to take this work, this kind of music that I'm trying to do. Here is a way to integrate a drum kit, and include some of the punch and energy of rock-and-roll, and get it with a Latin swing—here is a pointer of how to do this. It didn't always work, but a little light went on in my head in the middle of the show telling me that something was happening here.

At the end of the whole show, after the last encore, the brass section marched to the front of the stage playing "Happy Birthday," and the audience started singing along as well. It was a complete surprise.

Nico Gomes [assistant production manager] got bitten when he walked close to a "police" dog that a cop was holding. The dog lunged out and took a chunk out of his leg. Nico yelled at him (the cop) in English!

Today, upon arriving in Pôrto Alegre, after talking with a journalist on the telephone, an interview that Amelia had set up, there was a small press conference, an MTV thing set up in a small room downstairs.

The journalists asked me what I thought about the Brazilian audiences hearing me play samba. And I said that I thought a lot of the audiences I played to had probably never heard samba, judging by the Brazilian radio. There's a samba station in Rio, but you can't hear any Brazilian music, or very, very little in São Paulo and very, very little here in Pôrto Alegre. I said, "The Brazilian radio does not play Brazilian music. It plays rock-and-roll." They asked me why did I think that? Do I think it's the pressure of the multinationals?" I said, "Well, probably that, but probably also it's a class thing that samba, the local music, is considered low-class, the music of the poor." It's not considered refined. But rock-and-roll and jazz and other kinds of music are "refined," partly because they're foreign, and they are the music of the middle and upper classes. So all the kids aspire to listen to the music that might put their listening habits in another class. That night I dreamed I'm on a road that is somehow populated by hockey players (like air hockey). There are big slots in the road, on the left, right and center. Giant players move up and spin around and try to whack you. So I'm trying to advance up the road and avoid these players, sometimes crawling along a ditch on the side. Sometimes getting narrowly missed.

PORTO ALEGRE: WEDNESDAY

More chaos last night. Way past sound check time, the gear still has not arrived. Only 1,500 people have shown up due to the fact that the gig had been advertised in the paper as being on Tuesday or Wednesday. How can anyone expect an audience to appear if they don't tell them what day the show will be on?

So we make the decision to cancel tonight's date, to postpone it until tommorow. I hear that the gear has arrived. Everything is in, and we can go ahead. I say, "No, it's off." We get very emotional. I say, "No, it would be no soundcheck, still probably technically untogether. Very few people. We're all very tired. It would be very demoralizing. It would be an embarrassment. Let's forget it. Let's see if we can do it tomorrow."

The hitch is that postponing the date by one day would only work if we could get a Varig widebodied plane or Airbus to pick us up here in Pôrto Alegre and get us to Buenos Aires on Thursday, and if the promoter in Buenos Aires will arrange to get us through customs quickly there. If that can't happen, then we will have to leave today and forget playing here altogether. We await the answer.

PORTO ALEGRE: THURSDAY, MAY 17

Yesterday, in the afternoon I went with Marcia Garcia [tour manager and publicist] and some guy from the record company, WEA, here in Pôrto Alegre, to two radio stations so I could remind people that the show was on that night. It was the usual situation. The music portions of the radio stations, most of them, look like they rarely play any Brazilian music. All the posters were for Rolling Stones, Heavy Metal bands, whatever.

Later I ran into Cafe in his jogging outfit, and we talked. People had apparently spoken to him about my comments to the press about the Brazilian radio not playing Brazilian music. He said that he felt the same way and that he felt he had to leave Brazil to play Brazilian music! That it was very sad, people turning away from the riches of their own culture.

We passed a man selling herbs and leaves, some of them medicinal, on a table by the roadside. I bought two roots that Cafe said were very good for stress and general energy.

Went to the venue. Everything seemed more or less together. I suppose no music stands were to be had, because a couple of men with nails and saws and black paint were making music stands out of wood, for the horn players.

The place was probably the biggest place we've played. It's called the Gigantino or something. It's a basketball arena, indoors. It holds maybe ten thousand people. We were lucky if we got four thousand in there for the show, although it looked pretty good and the crowd made a good noise and they filled the floor. They were very, very enthusiastic.

This was the second show with Oscar. I went in earlier than usual with Oscar, Hector (the conga player), Cafe and Paquito, the pianist, and we just worked on the rhythms and some of the breaks and changes. Oscar still has a tendency to play the kit more than his Latin percussion.... Which is quite a change from what this band started off doing. But sometimes the combination of the two works very well. I am intrigued by his including an occasional kick drum or high-hat, and combining it with the Latin percussion. And on one song, I think it was "Dirty Old Town," he suggested using a songo rhythm for the choruses at the end, which Hector said sounded pretty good.

This rhythm (songo) and his way of playing the drum kit comes from him being closer to Cuba than to the New York Latin musicians. It has been said that the Cubans have created new hybrid beats like the songo and added drum kits to the Latin percussion, while the New York groups have stayed with what they played when they left Cuba around the time of the Revolution. Some say that the New York sound is purer. Many contemporary Cubans just say it sounds older, it sounds like it's been frozen in the instrumentation and the rhythms that were popular at that time.

Today is Saturday, the day after the first show in Buenos Aires. Friday morning I decided to tint my hair a little bit. I had bought some henna in Pôrto Alegre that said *preto* (black), and I proceeded to put the mud on my hair and let it sit for forty minutes. When I took it off, my hair was orange, red, black, gray, all sorts of colors. I panicked and went out to the nearest pharmacy and bought some black hair color, which turned out to be blacker and more permanent than I desired. I look more rock-and-roll than I have for a long time. Kind of punk and early Roy Orbison. But, hey, maybe it's all right.

The show went quite well. The audience was very enthusiastic. "Todo Cambia," the one song I sing in Spanish, got its best reception yet. I was so surprised I forgot some of the words. It's been a difficult song to get over. Its rhythm is Andean, not Caribbean or Brazilian, so it's a groove that is unfamiliar to everyone in the band. I first heard it performed by Mercedes Sosa, the incredible Argentine singer, and I'm aware that although the song's lyrics are not directly political, it is "about" resisting the repression that existed for so many years here. So the song obviously has a deep meaning for people here, which is one of the reasons I chose to include it in this leg of our tour.

BUENOS AIRES: SUNDAY

The town has large boulevards, plazas, beautiful old buildings, cafes, luncheonettes, a subway system, and a main shopping street. There are a few street musicians playing, Andean groups just like the ones in New York—absolutely identical! And, unique to here, I would imagine, a group of older men and women singing tangos in the pedestrian shopping mall. The man gesticulates to the musicians, to the sky, to himself, to an imaginary woman, even declaims some verses, not singing them, just speaking them as if he's talking to an imaginary person. I think they must be from a show of some sort, because their outfits are too "typical." They look like caricatures of tango musicians. He wears a black suit with a vest and a little Borsalino hat, as does another man who is standing to the side. They draw a fairly sizable crowd, which applauds after every number.

The audience was very, very enthusiastic Saturday, singing along

Saxophones filled out the wall of sound on Rei Momo.

on "Todo Cambia" and "Make Believe Mambo," jumping up and down a lot. It seemed more or less a sellout. The spirits in the band were good.

We want to do a second date in Santiago, now that there seems to be no possibility to do the date in Venezuela or in Salvador, Bahia. The Sunday night show went very well as well. A number of local musicians attended this show. Charley Garcia, Leon Giéco, Leda Valladares (the woman who has compiled a lot of the music of the Indians of the North in the countryside), a young musician from a group called Virus, and numerous others. Leon Giéco is the man who wrote the song "Carrito," which Pablo Milanes and Silvio Rodriguez sing in duet in a live recording I have. The song has also been recorded by Mercedes Sosa. I learned it as part of my Spanish class.

I was told that, a number of years ago, Leon took an abrupt change in the direction of his music, incorporating many of the regional musics of Argentina. He made a tour around the country, working with local musicians in small towns and villages, recording their music and sometimes collaborating with them recording his own songs. It was released as a TV special and two records. After that, he incorporated more regional flavors in his own compositions—mixing drums, percussion, bandoneon, violin and guitar.

BUENOS AIRES: MONDAY, MAY 21

We all meet up again. Leda Valladares presents me with a drum that is made by the Indians of the Andean north. It's a drum like those played on recordings she has made and recordings she has collected. She plays a little bit, right there in the hotel lounge, and begins to sing in a piercing, pinched voice typical of the mountain people.

Leon Giéco shows up, and he presents me with a *charango,* a small instrument like an eight-string *cavaquinho* (as a similar instrument is called in Brazil) or an eight-string ukulele. Apparently, the back of the instrument used to be made of an animal, like an armadillo, but now, due to the fact that these animals are becoming extinct, the back is made with a single piece of wood. He plays a little bit as well. It sounds beautiful. He shows me a small instruction book for the instrument.

Leda gives her impressions of the concert. She is excited and intrigued by the fact that many different kinds of music from dif-

128

ferent parts of Latin America are being woven together. She says that what I am doing is making bridges between these different regions and different cultures, and sewing them together in some way, making links where before there was kind of an isolation. It's all very flattering. This is coming from a woman who is about seventy years old and knows really nothing of pop music. She has spent a good part of her life in the mountains, collecting the music of the people there. My history, where I am from, Talking Heads, all mean nothing to her. She is speaking only from what she heard and what she has seen of the reaction of the people in Argentina.

A writer friend of Amelia's talks about the make-up of his band. He talks about the violin player in his band—that this man was refused a visa by the United States because he looked too Indian and they suspected him of God knows what. Leon himself narrowly escaped being one of the Disappeared during the military regime here. He was put in jail, and someone managed to get him out. He was allowed to go to live in Ann Arbor! And oddly enough that experience, and the music he heard then, sparked his interest in the indigenous music of his native Argentina. After a while, when things changed he could return. The same was also true of Mercedes Sosa. She went to live in Europe.

Thirty thousand people were Disappeared. Some were killed for political reasons, when The Generals disagreed with their politics. Others vanished apparently at random. Someone who played with a Brazilian group, a keyboard player, was Disappeared. They came in to perform, the keyboard player was snatched for no reason whatsoever (maybe he had long hair), and they never heard from him again. And these people are not even Argentine. It was much worse for those who lived here.

A Chilean group, Inti-Illuminati, had been forced into exile, when the U.S. helped overthrow the Allende government. They were sent on a state-sponsored European tour just before the overthrow of the government, sent by Allende because he could see that things were getting hot, and so he sent people out of the country. This band was not allowed to return for sixteen years. They can now joke about it, and say it was the longest tour they've ever been on. They thought they were going for two weeks to play in Italy, and they came back sixteen years later.

After we all go down by the River Plata for lunch, it's decided that

Singer Margareth Menezes, brought the crowd to their feet, performing her own songs, as a warm-up before Byrne came on stage.

we can go visit Mercedes Sosa at her apartment. Leon has called in advance, and she's welcomed us all to stop by for coffee. I am, of course, thrilled. One of the best singers in the world. And, of course, another one who was forced into exile during the military years in Argentina.

Mercedes Sosa talks about her upcoming dates, her past tours of Europe and the States. I tell her that I have seen her in New York. And she is happy that I am bringing this music, which is rarely heard in Argentina. She talks a little bit about the musicians in Brazil. She sings a number of songs of Chico Buarque, and she has a great love of Caetano Veloso. She sings a little bit of Caetano's song "Leonzinho." After another round of coffees, we all hug each other and say, "Goodbye, good afternoon."

I'm invited out to dinner with Jerry Massucci, the co-founder and head of Fania Records in New York, who has lived here now for a few years and a friend of his. Jerry talks about how the Latin music, salsa and Tropical music is virtually unknown here. He mentions that Morris Levy, the head of Tico Records and Roulette Records, a notorious and seminal figure in rock-and-roll and Latin music in the fifties and sixties, has just died. Many of the greatest artists in Latin music and Little Richard and lots of others were on Tico or Roulette in the early sixties.

We talk about what it's like being on the road with a large band. He has lots of stories to tell about crazy musicians, about bands that were high on one substance or another. They'd be great when they were on stage and totally uncontrollable off stage. They talk about tours they've done in South America that Jerry helped put together, which were equally or more chaotic than ours. Shows where, for one reason or another, the band couldn't or wouldn't go on, and the audience would start to destroy the stadium or the stage.

Then he told some stories about—I guess it was the late fifties, early sixties—a DJ in New York named Symphony Sid who used to have a radio program which, he said, all of the hospital attendants, elevator operators, everyone who was working at night, taxi drivers, would listen to. This program was the only means of promoting the Latin music in New York. [*Symphony Sid began by glomming onto emergent post-war bebop. He broadcast live from Birdland beginning in 1949, then went exclusively Latin by the end of the fifties. Lester Young wrote "Jumpin' With Symphony Sid" as a theme song.—JH*] Jerry told stories about audience request lines, where the people phoning in would make...deals over the air, saying, "Dear Joe: I'm waiting for my package," or whatever. That would be the "dedication." Those kind of things. Eventually, Symphony Sid went off the air. The nature of radio changed. It may be a little less corrupt in some ways, or maybe the corruption has become more formalized. It's a lot less exciting as well, and there seem to be fewer opportunities for these varied kinds of musical mixes to happen on the air.

SANTIAGO, CHILE

Today, Santiago is probably the most polluted city on earth. The Andes rise sharply against the city. We could see them from the hotel windows when we arrived. But by late afternoon, they are almost invisible, and they are very close. In fact, you can barely see a quarter of a mile through the haze. My throat hurts. People who have been outside say their eyes hurt.

This city has a hard-to-define or non-existent character. It's such a jumble of the old, the new, the temporary, the permanent. As someone said yesterday at lunch, "Buenos Aires and Argentina may look to Europe; we in Chile look to the United States as our model." That may explain some of this jumble.

The Muzak outside in the adjoining shopping mall is coordinated with the music inside the hotel. I make a seamless transition from the street to the shopping mall, into the hotel, and into the elevator and never lose a beat.

We are all whisked off to a TV studio at five o'clock, where we will be on live TV, a kind of Ed Sullivan Show, a variety show that airs that night. We'll be performing about four songs. And apparently, seventy percent of the country watches the show.

The actual show consists of us playing about two songs at the head and two songs at the tail. In the middle will be a magician, the contestants from the Miss Chile contest, a comedian, a short game show with some money prizes, and a kind of tango ballad group.

When it's time for our entrance, it's pitch dark backstage. We all stumble out onto the risers. Steve Sacks stumbles into an onstage fountain that is supposed to gush up behind the various Miss Chiles who will turn around on a large turntable. He is going to be playing these songs in very wet shoes.

We get through the first two songs. The reaction from the audience is very limited, to say the least. During the instrumental segments of both songs, parts of the audience begin to clap along, as if on cue, as if an applause sign or something had been switched on. Somehow, by the time we go on for the closing two songs, everything has changed. The audience has livened up; the house sound is happening, and the monitors are serviceable if not very good. It gets a tremendous reaction. Even the Miss Chile contestants, who are seated in the front row of the audience, get up and start clapping and dancing.

Earlier that evening, I visit the soundcheck and rehearsal of the group, Inti-Illuminati, the group that employs indigenous South American instruments and rhythms and songs of South America. Some of them are familiar with what we're doing; they admire what we're doing, feel that we have a common purpose. They play bits and fragments of songs. But they don't really do a rehearsal. They are unhappy with the monitor mix. It's nice to see somebody else having the same problems that we have.

Eventually, we get dropped off at a seafood restaurant—Lewis Kahn, Steve Sacks, Margareth, Mike Missiras, Brenda Dunlap, Peter Jennings and I are dropped off at a place called Something Coco. We seem to be recognized everywhere, as everyone has seen the TV program. It was reviewed in the next day's paper, and excerpts from the press conference were printed as well. In the reviews they made a funny comparison between myself and Xuxa, who opened the program on prerecorded videotape. She's number one, not just in Brazil, where she's from, but in other Latin American countries as well; she's done some recordings in Spanish, so now she's expanded into the Spanish market.

The restaurant is littered with phallic jokes. The bar has little knick-knacks, those little coffins that you open up and the corpse's dick pops up. Little things that you crank and dicks pop out of hidden slots. The men's room is lined with cartoons of guys with their penises hanging out. A snake-charmer being strangled by his own penis.

At the end of the meal, the maitre'd or owner wants to have his picture taken with us for his celebrity wall of photos, which we agree to. And after that, he gives us all silly hats to put on. A fez, a Nazi helmet, a Confederate Army hat, a tri-corner hat, a Chinese Mandarin hat, a Mongolian fur hat. At that point, all of us have had a few drinks, so it produces the desired effect. Everyone is trying on hats and taking pictures and getting a good laugh.

SANTIAGO: THURSDAY

The Santiago date was very, very well received by the audience. The technical end was—well, we got through it. But the audience was fantastic. "Todo Cambia," of course, went over particularly well in Santiago, being composed by a Chilean who wrote it when he was in exile. The audience lit their lighters and matches and sang along. A concert cliché that seemed genuine here. Some cried. All in all, it was very moving.

Afterwards, a few of us, Margareth, Hector, Peter Jennings, Oscar, Vincent and I, took a ten-minute walk to a place called the Salsatheq-ua, which is a very small club in a happening section of Santiago. Throughout most of our South American jaunt we heard very little local music, and if we did, it often sounded like a copy of North American styles. I was not the only one in the group to be disappointed. We had to make a real effort to ask for a record store that specialized in local sounds, or a club that had live regional music. Even this place, a Salsa discotheque, was not playing local music but recordings of Caribbean and New York groups. And their live band, as enjoyable as they were, played in those styles also.

Some of our guys sit in.... I'm too exhausted, so I dance with Magareth a little and walk back to the hotel.

SAN ANTONIO, TEXAS

The Alamo looks quite small, and inside all the tourists step slowly from exhibit to exhibit speaking in hushed tones. I find it disgusting. I see it as an historical example of ruthless North American aggression against Central America. Blatant land grabbing—move a few settlers into someone else's territory and eventually, with the help of a lot of soldiers, claim the land as your own. Disgusting behavior is being celebrated to the point where it is treated as a holy crusade. The Church of Rambo.

We've played Dallas, Austin, San Antonio and Denver, and tonight we play here in Santa Fe. It's beautiful. It's about seventy-five degrees; the air is clear, it's not too hot yet.

Bonny and I drive with Jo Harvey and Terry Allen to a church in the hills. The shrines inside are beautiful. On an altar across the front of the church, there is a row of candles, some of them for the Seven African Powers—the Orishas—with the names of the African gods and pictures of the Catholic saints on the candles. Virgins of Guadalupe. Babies dressed in woolen clothes.

In a side room, there are tons of homemade ex-votos. Thousands of hand-painted pictures of Jesus or the Virgin. Some in pencil, some on velvet, some with crayon. They are joined with family pictures, creches, medical bandages, old casts, Virgins made out of glitter, statues with beads, articles of clothing.

And then, in another anteroom, there is the healing dirt. The miracle dust. It's in a hole in the center of the floor and is reported to have healing properties. It looks like typical New Mexico dirt. People take little bits of the sand—or even whole bottles of it—and the hole magically refills itself. So they claim. Terry claims he has seen the gardener shovel sand in through the window.

Bonny, Malu and I are dropped off at the Paolo Solari amphitheater, the place where we're going to play. It is dug into the earth and almost invisible from ground level. Only a couple of the light towers stick up above the earth's surface. Even the stage is invisible. Due to the severe angle of the seats the audience will be right up against us. The front seats are about two yards from my singing position.

It goes great. One of the most exciting shows ever. Terry and Jo Harvey bring along Doug Wheeler, an L.A. light and space artist whose work I like.

LOS ANGELES: A FEW DAYS LATER

The Ventura date went fine. It was a beautiful old theater that had been converted into a dinner club. We went on just as the audience was having beers and having their coffee and desserts. I thought they'd all be too full to get up and dance, but we got them dancing by about

© F-STOP FITZGERALD

Margareth Menezes, vocalist on the Rei Momo tour, teaches the audience to samba.

the fourth or fifth song.

The next day we all did "The Tonight Show" in Los Angeles. Quite a surprise for us to be asked to be on Johnny Carson, a TV institution in the States for twenty-five years or so. It went without incident. Johnny was the host. That was nice. He doesn't often host his own show any more. All the technical people were very nice to us. The house band, Doc Severinson's band, was very nice to our guys, and they exchanged compliments. We wanted to do two songs; but I think we were squeezed out by the famous newsman, Peter Jennings, so we only got to play one. I was invited to chat with Johnny. I guess that's an honor.

The performance on the Carson Show was fine. Nothing extraordinary, but what do you expect for TV? It's a very artificial situation. It's hard to bang into the first number like it's the high point of your set. I suppose some performers are more practiced at projecting, through some kind of craft or tricks, a convincing display of energy on television. There's a craft and skill to being a regular talk show guest as well. There are some folks who seem to do nothing else but appear on these shows, and they seem to be very good at it, for whatever that's worth. They know, for instance, that you shouldn't make any quick, unexpected movements because you'll look like I do on TV, like a nervous bird.

We do two shows in L.A. The first at the Palladium, a ballroom similar to Roseland in New York, and the second at the Greek Theater, an outdoor place that holds about five or six thousand. We don't quite fill it. These shows go over really well.

I think some of the Warner's people may have been convinced that, yes, I am serious about this. I have continued touring behind it; and it just gets better and better, and they realize they shouldn't wait for another Talking Heads record. Now that the last couple of dates on the tour have finally come around, the record company has finally realized that this is what I am committed to, not to Talking Heads at the moment.

Margareth and I appear on Tom Schnabel's radio show on public radio. Diblo Dabala is there too, just leaving. I'm thrilled to meet him, one of my favorite guitarists. I zip over to Warner Brothers in Burbank and talk with one of the presidents of Warner Brothers. He seems to think that I made some creative blunders on my record, that the fusion of Latin and pop wasn't quite complete. If I could somehow make it more complete, it would be more accessible, and it would get over to a wider public. He may be right. He may not be right. At any rate, I don't want to straighten out the rhythms. Now, with the addition of Oscar, we have a slightly more "familiar" sound, a drum kit, and it has added a little more of the rock power and muscle to the sound.

The show at the Greek goes over really well. The band plays great. I have paid and arranged for, with Marcia's help, a small party for the band and crew, this being our last gig of the regular tour, at a club called Spice in Hollywood. It's not much, but I guess it's the thought that counts. At least I hope it counts for something.

NEW YORK: A FEW DAYS LATER

Back here in New York, I have a little chat with Amelia from Buenos Aires, who calls up and says that there's been lots of press, people keep talking about the shows in Buenos Aires. Musicians are divided in their opinions about it. It has created a little bit of controversy. Which is good. She feels very positive about it, that it's opened some doors and stirred things up a little bit.

It's odd not being on the road. Is this home? Do I live here? It's a funny place.

TIMELINE

Discography

With Talking Heads

1977   *TALKING HEADS : 77* (Sire, 1977). The original foursome, fresh from their post-grad nights at CBGB's, recorded songs that made everyday experience the hot topic for new rock, with titles as flatfooted as the album's ("New Feeling," "Tentative Decisions," "The Book I Read"). Another trademark was a twisted take on politics ("Don't Worry About the Government") that earned them the "young Republicans of rock" moniker. Highlight: the earliest version of "Psycho Killer." The back cover photograph is the first of several showing the band in basic police line-up stance, staring deadpan at the viewer.

1978   *MORE SONGS ABOUT BUILDINGS AND FOOD* (Sire). Brian Eno both co-produced and played (synthesizers, piano, guitar, percussion, and background vocals), with the band. The album announced an expanded ambition with typical Talking Heads songs ("Artists Only," "The Good Thing," "Found A Job") balanced by a killer cover of Al Green's "Take Me To The River." The album jacket is a Byrne concept graphic: a life-size photomosaic of the bandmembers made of 529 close-up Polaroids;

the back is a photomosaic of the United States made up of 569 photos taken from space. The *Little Creatures* album and the film *True Stories* would make Talking Heads's interest in American culture more explicit.

1979   *FEAR OF MUSIC* (Sire). Packaged in a cardboard simulation of industrial rubber matting, this album upped the urgency ante to something like an aural emergency alert. Again produced by Eno and the band, it ranges from Dadaist Hugo Ball's nonsense rants set to music ("I Zimbra") to the lovely, wistful "Heaven" ("A place where nothing ever happens"). But the theme song is the astonishing "Life During Wartime," a son-of-Psycho-Killer survivalist narrative erected on a driving groove that happens to be the best pre-*Terminator* description of the future according to Reagan.

1980   *REMAIN IN LIGHT* (Sire). Eno's last stint as producer adds more color via guest cameos (Robert Palmer, Nona Hendryx, Adrian Belew, Jon Hassell). Everybody switches instruments, percussion plays around every note, and tunes are more thickly textured than ever, built up from layers and layers of tracks. The killer song: "Once in a Lifetime," the beginning of Byrne's televangelist fixation. As if freed by the adoption of an emotional role, Byrne's singing starts to loosen up. The album's cover graphics—solarized faces of the band and a logo with the "A's" turned upside down—mark the start of a fruitful design relationship with Tibor Kalman's style-setting M & Co.

1982   *THE NAME OF THIS BAND IS TALKING HEADS* (Sire). Composed of live versions of the group's favorite numbers up until 1981, this album was the first hint that performance was becoming a major focus, with contributions by musicians who would later become part of the expanded band.

1983   *SPEAKING IN TONGUES* (Sire). The musical pinnacle of Talking Heads featured an expanded band—Alex Weir, Nona Hendryx, Dolette MacDonald, Steve Scales, Bernie Worrell—and a host of guest musicians loading the sound

Byrne solos with Talking Heads at the Warfield Theater in San Francisco.

to the limit. With only trace residues of Eno's high concepts (the record was produced by the band), *Tongues* was free to groove, and soar it does. Another hit that sounds like no other ("Burning Down the House"), a lyrically nonsensical but musically rocking song ("Girlfriend is Better"), and some skewed funk ("Swamp") make this collection one of those emblematic anthologies of an era's attitudes. Robert Rauschenberg designed a multilayered plastic package with dial-a-graphic capabilities which was beautiful but less than practical; it was difficult to produce, made the record cost too much, and tended to fall apart, but was still a remarkable effort to marry art and the commerce of pop. Byrne eventually created an Africanesque cover drawing as a substitute.

1984   *STOP MAKING SENSE* (Sire). The soundtrack for the documentary film of the same name includes jamming live versions of "Psycho Killer," "Burning Down the House," "Once in a Lifetime," "Life During Wartime," and "Take Me To The River," among others. Comes with an informative booklet illustrating the storyboarding and shooting of the movie.

1985   *LITTLE CREATURES* (Sire). Back to basics: the foursome is featured in a journey back into the heart of Talking Heads. Nonsequitur lyrics, lumpy rhythms, and alternating moods of childlike play and grown-up disconnection make this record one of the more unsettling of the band's many unbalancing acts. The single "Road to Nowhere" put it all into one tune, a Cajun-flavored, gospelish, anthem to what? The cover painting, by Georgia "outsider" artist Reverend Howard Finster, features drawings of the band in a fantastical paradise; on the back, the band repeats their standard police lineup pose, this time dressed up in gaudy duds and deader-than-usual stares.

1986   *TRUE STORIES* (Sire). There are two versions; one contains Talking Heads's versions of selected songs from the film, the other contains the film's instrumental music. On the former, the band's whole-hearted foray into American vernacular—

country, gospel, Tex-Mex—makes for an exuberant, straight-ahead sound. A minor gem: the heavy metal screech of "Love For Sale," featuring Frantz's killer drumming. On the latter, the catchall melange of styles—disco, Muzak, classical quartet, norteño, movie-symphonic—provides a more naked look than usual at Byrne's synthesizing methods.

1988   *NAKED* (Sire). And that it is—Talking Heads is exposed in an album of curiously undistinctive songs. Although there are moments ("Mr. Jones," a dig at Dylan; "Blind"), the album reeks of "Why?" Unable to answer that question sufficiently, this became the band's last recording to date.

1992   *POPULAR FAVORITES* (Sire). A two-disc anthology with some of Talking Heads's greatest hits, plus six previously unreleased songs.

© F-STOP FITZGERALD

Byrne during a mellower vocal on Rei Momo.

1989   *REI MOMO* (Luaka Bop/Sire). Latin music 101 for Anglos.
        With Byrne's earnestness and an impressive roster of collab-
        orators (Willie Colon, Johnny Pacheco, Celia Cruz), the
        album is a fruitful lesson in multicultural exchange and trans-
        formation, a point not understood by carpers who cried,
        "dilettante," upset by its lack of "authenticity." This was pre-
        cisely the problem Byrne was not addressing. More to the
        point is a kind of awkwardness in the grooves, as if two
        unlikely partners were made to dance together by their par-
        ents. One rouser, "Don't Want to Be Part of Your World,"
        breaks out. The live shows, not available on recording,
        showed the potential in the material.

1991   *THE FOREST* (Luaka Bop/Sire). Byrne coins "industrial sym-
        phonic" as a new style: Wagner meets Fritz Lang in the
        nineties. The soundtrack to a Robert Wilson stage produc-
        tion, the score has been performed in concert where, sur-
        prisingly, it held its own, apart from Wilson's indelible the-
        atrical images.

        FORESTRY : *AVA (NU WAGE REMIX)* A dance mix single from the
        symphonic suite, and a curious oddity.

1992   *UH-OH* (Luaka Bop/Sire/Warner Bros.). From its title, echo-
        ing Talking Heads's first song on their first album ("Uh-Oh,
        Love Comes to Town") to its twisty lyrics and even twistier
        rhythms, this sounds more like Talking Heads than did the
        band itself on *Naked*. The Latin coloration is more organic
        and integrated, Byrne's songwriting seems right on the mark,
        and his singing continues to loosen up.

Byrne with the chorus line during the taping of the Rei Momo video.

1981   *MY LIFE IN THE BUSH OF GHOSTS*, with Brian Eno
        (Sire/WarnerBros.). The album takes its attitude, as well as
        its title, from Nigerian novelist Amos Tutuola's haunting
        novel, a nightmarish tale about a small boy facing the terrors
        of the bush alone. The "bush" here is a postmodern electronic
        jumble of overheard and sampled voices and sounds.
        Sermons, Muslim chants, radio call-in talkers, and exorcisms
        are set to a mostly percussive background. One of those way-
        ahead-of-its-time creations that is actually more interesting
        now than when first released.

1986   "Liquid Days" and "Open the Kingdom," lyrics for two songs
        with music by Philip Glass, on Glass's *Songs from Liquid Days*
        (CBS Records) anthology. Other contributors included
        Laurie Anderson, Suzanne Vega and Paul Simon. The Roches'
        lovely harmonies make the non-sequitur lyrics of "Liquid
        Days" ache with meaning, while "Open the Kingdom" is a
        thundering church anthem, a neo-Martin Luther call to spir-
        itual arms.

© F-STOP FITZGERALD

Byrne and Margareth Menezes harmonize.

1982   *MUSIC AND RHYTHM*, (1982). An early world beat compilation by the World Music of Arts and Dance outfit (WOMAD), included Byrne's "His Wife Refused", one of the African-inflected tunes from *The Catherine Wheel.*

1989   *LIKE A GIRL I WANT YOU TO KEEP COMING*, (Giorno Poetry Systems). "Song for The Trees (or) I Know Sometimes The World is Wrong" was an outtake given to one of John Giorno's ambitious, eclectic, and aggressively avant-anthologies (proceeds to fight AIDS).

1990   *RED HOT & BLUE*, (Chrysalis). "Don't Fence Me In" was his contribution of skewed Cole Porter to an album of the same.

A contemplative Byrne between numbers.

1981   THE CATHERINE WHEEL (Sire/Warner Bros.). A score for Twyla Tharp's epic evening-length dance-theater work, with Brian Eno and John Chernoff. Interesting now for its nascent and pervasive African influence. One killer song: "Big Business" (heard on *Stop Making Sense*).

1984-85   Main title theme for ALIVE FROM OFF-CENTER (first season, 1984-85). A musical logo ditty for PBS's avant-film showcase, the squib showed that Byrnisms could go commercial, if he cared.

1985   MUSIC FOR THE KNEE PLAYS (ECM/Sire/Warner Bros.). For a stage collaboration with Robert Wilson and Suzushi Hanayagi, Byrne turned New Orleans brass band music (inspired by the Dirty Dozen Brass Band) on its head. The quixotic tunes are linked by typically oblique Byrne-scripted anecdotes.

1986   SOUNDS FROM TRUE STORIES (Sire/Warner Bros.). Just what it says.

1987   THE LAST EMPEROR (Virgin), directed by Bernardo Bertolucci. Byrne contributed one-third of a score (Cong Su and Ryuichi Sakamoto did the rest) that won an Academy Award, and deservedly so. Although Byrne set out to avoid *chinoiserie,* his songs sound like ancient oriental melodies filtered through postmodern minimalism. Some of his most haunting music, for a film about ghosts.

1989   MARRIED TO THE MOB (Reprise/Warner Bros.), directed by Jonathan Demme. Byrne contributed incidental music to the film, but the soundtrack consists of an anthology of musicians and groups, some of whom have been associated with him (Ziggy Marley , Tom Tom Club and Eno).

DEAD END KIDS (unreleased), the soundtrack for the film version of the stage play by JoAnne Akalaitis.

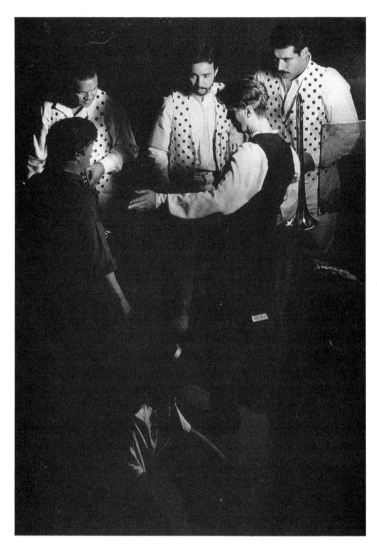

Byrne directing the horn section during the taping of the Rei Momo video.

1982   *MESOPATAMIA,* B-52s

1983   *WAITING,* Fun Boy 3

1990   *ELEGIBO,* Margareth Menezes (Two tracks: *Canto pra Subir* and *Abra a Boca*)

PRODUCER (Luaka Bop label)

1989   *BELEZA TROPICAL* (Brazil Classics 1)

1989   *O SAMBA: SAMBA & PAGODE* (Brazil Classics 2)

1990   *THE BEST OF TOM ZE: MASSIVE HITS.* (Brazil Classics 4)

1991   *FORRÓ, ETC: MUSIC FROM THE BRAZILIAN NORTHEAST.* (Brazil Classics 3)

1991   *GREATEST HITS OF SILVIO RODRIGUEZ: CANCIONES URGENTES.* (Cuba Classics 1).

1991   *INCREDIBLE DANCE HITS OF THE 60'S AND 70'S: DANCING WITH THE ENEMY* (Cuba Classics 2).

1992   *A.R. KANE: AMERICANA*

1992   *DANCE RAJA DANCE: THE SOUTH INDIAN FILM MUSIC OF VIJAYA ANAND* (Asia Classics 1).

The itinerary and schedule as the Rei Momo tour heads to Japan.

1984   *STOP MAKING SENSE* (Cinecom). Concert film conceived from a stage show, directed by Jonathan Demme. With Talking Heads.

1989   *TALKING HEADS VS. TELEVISION.* A collaboration with BBC Channel Four.

DIRECTOR

1986   *TRUE STORIES.* Co-written with Beth Henley and actor-director Stephan Tobolowsky. Also appeared in film.

1988   *STORYTELLING GIANT.* Compilation of Talking Heads's videos, seven directed by Byrne.

1989   *APRIL 16, 1989.* A two-and-one-half minute film, created with David Wild.

1989   *ILÉ AIYÉ (HOUSE OF LIFE).* Documentary about the Candomblé religion and its rituals, filmed in the Bahia region of Brazil.

1992   *GIRLS* and *SHE'S MAD.* Videos for the *Uh-Oh* album.

PRODUCER

1981   *AMERICA IS WAITING.* Film, directed by Bruce Conner.

1989   *UMBA BARA UMA.* Animated film-video for *Beleza Tropical,* directed by Susan Young.

ACTOR

SURVIVAL GUIDE. An original play for television written by Beth Henley, directed by Jonathan Demme.

Byrne discusses a scene with the director of photography during the taping of Rei Momo.

EXHIBITIONS

1990   *REPRODUCED AUTHENTIC.* (Group show, Gallerie Via Eight,
        Tokyo, Japan)

1991   *BEYOND JAPAN: A PHOTO THEATER.* (Group show, Barbican Art
        Gallery, London, England)

PUBLICATIONS

1990   *ARTFORUM*, ("We eat we are eaten," December).

1990   *PARKETT*, (Insert, No. 23)

1992   *APERTURE*, ("Our Town", No. 127).